FAST SPEAKING WOMAN

Chants & Essays

ANNE WALDMAN

POCKET POETS SERIES NO. 33

CITY LIGHTS BOOKS
San Francisco

© 1975, 1978, 1996 by Anne Waldman
All Rights Reserved
New expanded edition, 1996
10 9 8 7 6 5 4 3 2

Cover design: Rex Ray
Cover photograph: Sheyla Baykal, 1974
Book design: Nancy J. Peters
Typography: Harvest Graphics

Library of Congress Cataloging-in-Publication Data

Waldman, Anne, 1945–
    Fast speaking woman ; chants & essays / Anne Waldman. —
New expanded ed.
        p.   cm. — (Pocket poets series : no. 33)
    Expanded ed. of: Fast speaking woman & other chants. 1975.
    ISBN 0-87286-318-6
    I. Waldman, Anne, 1945– Fast speaking woman & other chants.
  II. Title.
PS3573.A4215F3   1996
811'.54 — dc20   98-1715
                                    CIP

City Lights Books are available to bookstores through our
primary distributor: Subterranean Company, P.O. Box 160,
265 S. 5th St., Monroe, OR 97456. 541-847-5274. Toll-free
orders 800-274-7826. FAX 541-847-6018. Our books are also
available through library jobbers and regional distributors. For
personal orders and catalogs, please write to City Lights Books,
261 Columbus Avenue, San Francisco, CA 94133.

CITY LIGHTS BOOKS are edited by Lawrence Ferlinghetti and
Nancy J. Peters and published at the City Lights Bookstore,
261 Columbus Avenue, San Francisco, CA 94133.

A Note On This Edition

I took the opportunity with this twentieth-anniversary expanded edition of *Fast Speaking Woman* to add — around the original pieces (published in two editions, 1975 and 1978) — work selected for the most part from a ten-year span (1973–1983) that accorded with the primary text, & also seemed relevant & resonant with the notion of "chant" manifested herein. Some pieces were unearthed from old files & notebooks and have never been published before. "Billy Work Peyote" and "Crack In The World" appeared first in *Skin Meat Bones,* Coffee House Press (1985), and in the spirit of this book seemed important to include. "Verses for the New Amazing Grace" is more recent, composed in response to Ed Sanders' call for a contribution to a lengthy choral collaborative epic. I also wanted to intersperse with the poems three unpublished essays from the mid-eighties, culled from journals & teaching notes. One focuses on the history & occasion of the title poem specifically, the others continue the discussion of the oral tradition, travel as implicit in a poet's work, ethnopoetics, Tibetan Buddhism, feminism, performance, and other related topics. It is pleasure to have this chance to present a more ample compilation of some of the early "oral" work, which was seminal to my growth as a poet, as well as some contextual explication.

A.W.
The Jack Kerouac School of Disembodied Poetics
The Naropa Institute
Boulder, Colorado
January 1, 1996

Acknowledgments

The pieces in this book in various versions have appeared in the following magazines (many of them extinct now):

Adventures in Poetry, Big Sky, Bombay Gin, Changes, Chicago, Contact, The Coldspring Journal, Fag Rag - Gay Sunshine, Dark Ages Clasp the Daisy Root, Loka, Lords of Language, Napalm Health Spa, Poetry Review, The Shambhala Sun, Telephone, The World.

An early version of "Fast Speaking Woman" was first published by The Red Hanrahan Press. "Guardian & Scribe" appears in the Heaven Chapbook series. Several pieces have also been published in the books *Skin Meat Bones* and *Helping the Dreamer,* Coffee House Press, and are used by permission of the publisher.

A special thanks to Devorah Dettloff for her help with "'I Is Another': Dissipative Structures."

CONTENTS

Invocation	1
Fast Speaking Woman	3
"Fast Speaking Woman" & The Dakini Principle	35
Hag's Heart	43
I Bow At Bodhgaya	45
Red Hat Lama	47
Lines to a Celebrated Friend	50
A Book of Events	52
Talking Mushrooms	54
Billy Work Peyote	58
Spel Against Specious Ones	61
Battery	62
Pressure	64
Lady Tactics	69
Notorious	71
Musical Garden	72
Empty Speech	76
Queer Heart	80
Light & Shadow	81
What Takes: Methyl Isocyanate	88
Gypsy Nun	99
The Nun Abutsu	101
After Mirabai	102
I Guard The Woods	103
Lament You Are In This Mind Of	104

Battle Beast   110
Anarchy Reggae   112
Bardo Corridor   114
Verses for the New Amazing Grace   116
Pratitya Samutpada   118
Crack in the World   119
Guardian & Scribe   122
Millennium Sutra   124
& Sleep the Lazy Owl Of Night   126
"I Is Another": Dissipative Structures   127

INVOCATION

after Korinna

all the city is delighted with the
clear water of
my plaintive voice

—*Greek, 6th century*

I'm here to sing
the power of
poets & lovers
who lift their
hearts
in song

To modern daughters
in silk & leather,
long earrings
I sing

To sons
of any color

May you be roused
by a
fast-trembling
song

"Fast Speaking Woman" is indebted to Maria Sabina, the Mazatec Indian shamaness in Mexico, guiding persons in magic mushroom ceremony & is a reworking & coincidence of the same for all wandering spirits. Reading aloud as intended I can be more playful improvising new words & sound thus expanding the territory I'm in. The piece began as a travel meditation during a trip to South America, continued back in NYC, then later in India. It kept growing. Sabina died in the mid-1980s.

FAST SPEAKING WOMAN

"I is another"
                    —Rimbaud

because I don't have spit
because I don't have rubbish
because I don't have dust
because I don't have that which is in air
because I am air
let me try you with my magic power:

     I'm a shouting woman
     I'm a speech woman
     I'm an atmosphere woman
     I'm an airtight woman
     I'm a flesh woman
     I'm a flexible woman
     I'm a high-heeled woman
     I'm a high-style woman
     I'm an automobile woman
     I'm a mobile woman
     I'm an elastic woman
     I'm a necklace woman
     I'm a silk-scarf woman
     I'm a know-nothing woman
     I'm a know-it-all woman
     I'm a day woman
     I'm a doll woman

I'm a sun woman
I'm a late-afternoon woman
I'm a clock woman
I'm a wind woman
I'm a white woman
I'M A SILVER-LIGHT WOMAN
I'M AN AMBER-LIGHT WOMAN
I'M AN EMERALD-LIGHT WOMAN

I'm an abalone woman
I'm the abandoned woman
I'm the woman abashed, the gibberish woman
the aborigine woman, the woman absconding
the Nubian Woman
the antediluvian woman
the absent woman
the transparent woman
the absinthe woman
the woman absorbed, the woman under tyranny
the contemporary woman, the mocking woman
the artist dreaming inside her house

I'm the gadget woman
I'm the druid woman
I'm the Ibo woman
I'm the Yoruba woman
I'm the vibrato woman
I'm the rippling woman
I'm the gutted woman
I'm the woman with wounds

I'm the woman with shins
I'm the bruised woman
I'm the eroding woman
I'm the suspended woman
I'm the woman alluring
I'm the architect woman
I'm the trout woman
I'm the tungsten woman
I'm the woman with the keys
I'm the woman with the glue

I'm a fast speaking woman

                        water that cleans
                        flowers that clean
                        water that cleans as I go

I'm a twilight woman
I'm a trumpet woman
I'm the raffia woman
I'm a volatile woman
I'm the prodding woman
I'm the vagabond woman
I'm the defiant woman
I'm the demented woman
I'm the demimonde woman
I'm the woman deracinated, the woman destroyed
the detonating woman, the demon woman

I'm the lady of the acacias
I'm the lady with the rugs

I'm the accomplished woman
I'm the woman who drives
I'm the alabaster woman
I'm the egregious woman
I'm the embryo woman

I'm the girl under an old-fashioned duress

I'm a thought woman
I'm a creator woman
I'm a waiting woman
I'm a ready woman
I'm an atmosphere woman
I'm the morning-star woman
I'm the heaven woman

   that's how it looks when you go to heaven
   they say it's like softness there
   they say it's like day
   they say it's like dew

I'm a lush woman

I'm a solo woman
I'm a sapphire woman
I'm a stay at home woman
I'm a butterfly woman
I'm a traveling woman
I'm a hitchhike woman
I'm a hitching-post woman

I'm a sun woman
I'm the coyote woman
I won't be home
I'll be back

I'm a justice woman
it's not sadness
no, it's not a lie

I'm the Southern Cross woman
I'm a moon woman
I'm a day woman
I'm a doll woman
I'm a dew woman
I'm a lone-star woman
I'm a loose-ends woman
I'm a pale-coast woman
I'm a mainstay woman

I'm a rock woman
I'm a horse woman
I'm a monkey woman
I'm a chipmunk woman
I'm a mountain woman
I'm a blue mountain woman
I'm a marsh woman
I'm a jungle woman
I'm a tundra woman
I'm the lady in the lake
I'm the lady in the sand

water that cleans
flowers that clean
water that cleans as I go

I'm a bird woman
I'm a book woman
I'm a devilish clown woman
I'm a holy-clown woman
I'm a whirling-dervish woman
I'm a whirling-foam woman
I'm a playful-light woman
I'm a tidal-pool woman
I'm a fast speaking woman

I'm a witch woman
I'm a beggar woman
I'm a shade woman
I'm a shadow woman
I'm a leaf woman
I'm a leaping woman
I'M A GREEN-PLANT WOMAN
I'M A GREEN-ROCK WOMAN
I'm a rest-stop woman

I'm a city woman

I long for the country

I get on the airplanes and fly away

I know how to work the machines!

8

I'm a sighing woman
I'm a singing woman
I'm a sleeping woman
I'm a muscle woman
I'm a music woman
I'm a mystic woman
I'm a cactus woman
it's not strange
no, it's not a lie

I'm the diaphanous woman
I'm the diamond-light woman
I'm the adamant woman
I'm the headstrong woman
I'm the tunnel woman
I'm the terrible woman
I'm the tree woman
I'm the trembling woman
I'm the treacherous woman
I'm the touchy woman

      flowers that clean
      water that cleans
      flowers that clean as I go

I'm an impatient woman
I've got the right of way
I'm the baby woman, I'll cry
I'm the wireless woman
I'm the nervous woman

I'm the wired woman
I'm the imperious woman
I'm the purple sky woman

I'M THE PURPLE-LIGHT WOMAN
I'M THE SPECKLED-LIGHT WOMAN
I'M THE SUGAR-LIGHT WOMAN
I'm the breathless woman
I'm the hurried woman
I'm the girl with the unquenchable thirst

                                  flowers that clean as I go
                                  water that cleans
                                  flowers that clean as I go

hey you there
hey you there, boss
I'm talking

I'm a jive-ass woman
I'm the callous woman
I'm the callow woman
I'm the clustered woman
I'm the dulcimer woman
I'm the dainty woman
I'm the murderous woman
I'm the discerning woman
I'm the dissonant woman
I'm the anarchist woman
I'm the Bantu woman

I'm the Buddha woman
I'm the baritone woman
I'm the bedouin woman

I'm the woman with taste
I'm the woman with coral

I'm the mushroom woman
I'm the phantom woman
I'm the moaning woman
I'm the river woman
I'm the singing river woman
I'm the clear-water woman
I'm the cleansing woman
I'm the clay woman
I'm the glazed woman
I'm the glass-eyed woman

I'm the stone woman
I'm the stone-tooth woman
I'm the woman with bones
I'm the fossil woman
I'm the soft flesh woman
I'm the doe-eyed woman

> that's how it looks when you go to heaven
> they say it's like softness there
> they say it's like land
> they say it's like day
> they say it's like dew

I'm the lonesome woman
the woman without a home
I'm the lithesome woman
the limber woman, the woman forbidden
the woman divided, the woman entangled
the woman caught between two continents
the woman dancing inside her house

I'm the contented woman
I'm the unrelenting woman
the unresolved woman
the woman with the treble
the soprano woman
the woman who roves
the woman riding in clover
the woman deliberating
the foraging woman
the phenomena woman
the woman who studies
the woman who names
the woman who writes
I'm the cataloguing woman

                water that cleans
                waters that run
                flowers that clean as I go

I'm the vendetta woman
I'm the inventive woman
I'm the invective woman

I'm the reflective woman
I'm the grave miscreant
I'm the molten matter
I'm the substratum
I'm the tumbleweed woman
I'm the half-breed
I'm the banyan tree woman
I'm the static woman
I'm the woman in classic pose

I'm the silk woman
I'm the cloth woman

I'M THE SILVER-CLOTH WOMAN
I'M THE GOLD-CLOTH WOMAN
I'M THE EMERALD-CLOTH WOMAN
I'm the weaving woman
I'm the woman with colorful thread
I'm the fiber woman
I'm the fleeing woman
the woman forgotten
the woman derailed
the tempestuous woman

I'm the woman who dreams
I'm the woman who exhales

I'm the night woman
I'm the black-night woman
I'm the night without a moon

I'm the angel woman
I'm the white-devil woman
I'm the green-skin woman
I'm the green-goddess woman
I'm the woman with arms
I'm the woman with wings
I'm the woman with sprouts
I'm the woman with leaves
I'm the branch woman
I'm the masked woman
I'm the deep-trance woman

I'm the meat woman
I'm the red-meat woman
I'm the fish woman
I'm the blue-fish woman
I'm the woman with scales
I'm the woman with fins
I'm the crawling woman
I'm the swimming woman
I'm the sun-fish woman
I'm the silver-fish woman

water that cleans
flowers that clean as I go

I'm the moss woman
I'm the velvet-moss woman
I'm the woman with vines
I'm the woman with thorns

I'm the needle woman
I'm the pine-needle woman
I'm the science woman
I'm the mistaken woman
I'm the inexorable woman
I'm the explorer woman

> that's how it looks when you go to heaven
> they say it's like softness there
> they say it's like land
> they say it's like day
> they say it's like dew

I'm the impoverished woman
I'm the heavy-belly woman
I'm the woman with hair
I'm the woman with child
I'm the heathen woman
I'm the hermaphrodite woman
I'm the iridescent woman
I'm the hazardous woman
I'm the precipice woman
I'm the insouciant woman
I'm the jasmine woman
I'm the jaguar woman
I'm the Inca woman
I'm the woman with the facade
I'm the woman with the sparks

I'm the taxi woman
I'm the tactile woman
I'm the ductile woman
I'm the taciturn woman
I'm the fierce woman
I'm the Jupiter woman
I'm the tiger woman
I'm the woman with claws
I'm the woman with fangs
I'm the closed-circuit woman
I'm the muddy-bank woman
I'm the big-footed woman
I'm the big-hearted woman
I'm the water-pool woman
I'm the shimmering woman

I'm flowers radiating light

I'm the heavy-paint woman
I'm the patina woman
I'm the matinee woman
I'm the Neanderthal woman
I'm the automaton woman
I'm the decadent woman
I'm the opulent woman

water that cleans
flowers that clean
water that cleans as I go

I'm the beads woman
I'm the stone-beads woman
I'm the money-belt woman
I'm the woman with the passport
I'm the immigrant woman

I'm the woman with the weight on her shoulders
I'm the woman with the weight on her back
I'm the old woman
I'm the stooped-over woman
I'm the barefoot woman
I'm the dark-eyed woman
I'm the raven-dark woman
I'm the jet-black woman

I'm the slippery-eel woman
I'm the facile woman
I'm the princess woman
I'm the serpent woman
I'm the ecliptic woman
I'm the sine-wave woman
I'm the sliding woman

                                        waters that clean
                                        flower that cleans
                                        waters that clean as I go

I'm the sensible woman
I'm the senseless woman
I'm the pink-dawn woman

I'm the mist-dawn woman
I'm the mysterious woman
the woman demystified
the woman divulged
the apocalypse woman
I'm the plexiglass woman
I'm the rash woman
I'm the hushed woman
I'm the caustic woman
I'm the resonating woman
I'm the altercating woman
the ambidextrous woman
the ambiguous woman
I'm the effusive woman
I'm the ancipital woman
I'm the woman in the mirror
I'm the woman in the museum
I'm a fast speaking woman

I'm the ameliorating woman
I'm the Marabout woman
I'm the indolent sylph
I'm the frugal handmaiden
I'm the harridan
I'm the trickster
I'm the minx
I'm the shy courtesan
I'm the frau
I'm the woman with the wares
I'm the woman with the whims

I'm the woman with the hems
I'm the woman with the volts
I'M THE POET DREAMING INSIDE HER HOUSE

I'm the tautological woman
I'm the technological woman
I'm the tally sheet woman
I'm the dallying woman

> water that cleans
> flowers that clean
> waters that clean as I go

I'm the hieratic woman
I'm the hermetic woman
I'm the harvesting woman
I'm the cloistered woman
I'm the prismatic woman
I'm the manic woman
I'm the magic woman

I'm the fleeting woman
I'm the floating woman
I'm the flotsam woman
I'm the gypsy woman
I'm the rain woman
I'm the rainy-season woman
I'm the lady from Twenty-nine Palms

I'm the inestimable woman I'll convert yr piastres to gold

I'm the Infanta, I'll get my way

I'm the disdainful woman
I'm the declaiming woman
I'm the thwarted woman
I'm the turgid woman
I'm the Tuscarora woman
I'm the farsighted woman
I'm the wry woman

       I'm the circular woman the woman
       who returns

          water that flows
          flowers that clean
          water that flows as I go

I'm the Parnassian woman
I'm the Parsee woman
I'm the monophobic woman
I'm the perfunctory woman
I'm the percussive woman
I'm the domestic woman
I'm the vigilante woman
I'm the chastising woman
I'm the Shakti
I'm the errant woman
I'm the variegated woman

I'm the woman with the clout

I'm the woman with the refrain

> flowers that clean as I go
> water that cleans
> flowers that clean as I go

I'm the raised-on-jazz woman
I'm the syncopated woman
I'm the woman at the keyboard
I'm the woman-turns-her-neck-around
I'm the clapping woman
I'm the strapping woman
I'm the back seat woman

I'm the crusader woman with teapot, bedroll, yellow
plastic water bottle & green turban shouting
Insh'allah on route to El Ayon—reclaim my
Sahara *Insh'allah!*

I'm the old old Polish woman raking & gathering
leaves mid-October just outside Chicago

I'm the woman scribbling on paper bag sitting by
Hudson, hat slouched over squint in autumn sun

I'm the pinched-face lady in Montreal serving you
up a tasty meal

I'm the woman standing in the shadow
the Navaho in velvet

I'm the visceral woman
I'm the Valkyrie
I'm the vermilion woman
the pivoting woman
the Vesuvian woman
I'm the vexed woman
I'm the woman put a hex on you
I'm the concealing woman
I'm the babbling woman
I'm the baksheesh baksheesh baksheesh woman
I'm the bankrupt woman
I'm the bargaining woman
I'm the barracuda woman
I'm the bellicose woman
I'm the benevolent woman
I'm the petulant woman
I'm the aimless woman
I'm the average woman
I'm the woman adoring
the woman adulterated
I'm the acetate woman
The acetylene woman

                    water that cleans
                    flowers that clean
                    water that cleans as I run

I'm the lone assassin I'll sit in my cell
I'm the inflamed woman ready to burn
I'm the notorious infidel

I'm the agent provocateur
I'm the infectious woman whose energy catches on
I'm the huckster woman just down the street
I'm the woman with the rings
I'm the woman with histrionics
I'm the vixen
the woman in the hovel
the woman on the dole

I'm the regenerative woman
I'm the woman strapped to the machine
I'm the reptile woman I'll grow back my limbs
I'm the reproachful woman I'll never forget
I'm the plutonium woman make you glow for a
    quarter of a million years!

I'm the Hottentot woman
I'm the hot-rod woman
I'm the hostile woman
I'm the equinox woman

            that's how it looks when you go to heaven
            they say it's like softness there
            they say it's balanced there
            they say it's like land like day like dew

I'm the monophonic woman
I'm the setaceous woman
I'm the moonlit woman in silence under trees
I'm the touchstone woman

23

I'm the woman with the vitamins
I'm the woman with the keys
I'm the woman with the delays
I'm the woman with the maize
I'm the woman who breathes in
I'm the woman who sails

I'm the redundant woman
I'm the incumbent woman
the woman askew, the woman amok
the amorous woman
the malachite woman
the hidden cave woman
THE WOMAN INSPIRED INSIDE HER HOUSE!

I'm the volcano woman
I'm the pressured woman
I'm the bituminous woman
I'm the slimy-fuel woman
I'm the bright-fire woman
I'm the fire-eater woman
I'm the spaced-out woman
I'm the hemmed-in woman
I'm the woman with the walking shoes
I'm the woman with the straw hat

I'm a fast speaking woman
I'm a fast-rolling woman

I'm a rolling-speech woman
I'm a rolling-water woman

I KNOW HOW TO SHOUT
I KNOW HOW TO SING
I KNOW HOW TO LIE DOWN

II

woman never under your thumb, says
skull that was a head, says
bloodshot eyes, says

I'm the Kali woman the killer woman
women with salt on her tongue

fire that cleans
fire that catches
fire burns hotter as I go

woman traded in her secrets never, says
woman reversed the poles, says
woman never left America to know this
but she did, says, she did leave

woman combs snakes out of her hair
woman combs demons out of her hair

woman lies down with the cobra
   then meditates under cobra canopy

woman had a bone in her throat, says
was it yours? says
she admits she has a taste for you, says
   she's cannibal woman, Kali woman

woman's tongue once split in ten directions
one: I'm a savage woman
two: I'm the rutting woman
three: I'm the fire dancer with coal-black feet
four: I'm the old-time thinker
five: poseur woman
six: I'm the redacteur
seven: auteur
eight: I haunt you with my songs
nine: I was the nun
   now I am bound by desire again
ten: I'm the *cittipatti* woman
   the dancing-skull woman

mouth is moving, says
skull-mouth moving, says
says these things
says terrible things as I go

mouth is gaping
tongue is bleeding
everywhere suffering, as I go

I'm the celebrity woman
I'm the luminary woman
I'm the standout woman
I'm the braggart woman
I'm the shrew at the window woman
I'm the stigma woman
the beaten woman
the disgraced woman
hag woman
where will I go?

who will have me?

water clean me
water clean me, as I go

I'm the camouflaged woman
I'm the assuaged woman
I'm the ravenous woman
I'm the Kali Yuga woman
high-pitched woman
not a trifling woman
hissing woman

I'm the woman with the fangs
I'm the woman with the guns
I'm the woman with tomes
I'm the book woman
I'm the stolen book woman

fire that burns as I go

woman was in the world was walking
woman was singing sounding the day away
sounds like a cranky old machine, someone said
(that someone was a mean man, mean child-man)
but she just ignored the cranky old machine part
& went on her way

woman took her haughty self out of the sky
she had a nose that tall
how tall?
that!
& stuck up it was
mincy mincy mincy mincy she cried
mincy mincy mincy
she was burning all right
her house (the one she carried on her head) was afire

I'm the woman never made a fool of
woman who hides her heart
woman hidden in long sleeves
    sleeves of green & gold
I'm the woman shelved one night
    while he beds down with the deer
I'm the woman wandering the forest
    tilt moon
    full moon lights up a honey eye
    half moon he returns
I'm the woman waiting

28

the woman counting moments
a moment never existed & he walks in
I'm the woman who scribes this text
     long after the animals lie down
chopping wood outside the retreat hut
stoking the fire with my little stick
a candle lit to light a teacher's face
I learn by books
I learn by singing
I recite the chant of one hundred syllables
I write down my messages to the world
the wind carries them invisibly,
     staccato impulses to the world

I'm the woman stirring the soup pot
the woman who makes circles
     with her arm
stirring, singing this song about the
     Woman-Who-Does-Things
many actions complete themselves
& repeat
she does this
I'm the woman who does these things
many actions carry words
I say them, woman-who-signifies
I light the fire
I sit like a Buddha
I feed the animals outside the door
I blow out the lamp

I'm the woman traveling inside her head
I'm the woman on the straw mat
I bewitch the stars to my heart
    points of light, arrows to my heart
pierce me as I sleep

I'm the night woman
I'm the terrible-night woman
I travel to steal your lover
    to steal your food, to take your words

I'm the day woman
I'm the doll woman
I'm the dew woman

day woman mends & organizes
doll woman sits & stares
dew woman is moist to the touch

I'm the Amoghasiddhi woman
I'm activity demon
I wait for him
I walk away
busy woman to light up the day!

don't touch me I'm hurrying hurrying
fierce light of day he doesn't exist
mayhem on the next block a proletarian urge
& old tones deep from his gut I shut ears to
hold back, hold back

I'm the woman shouting "Hold"
I'm running down the street now
shout: "Hold, hold"

& old tones hold back ears sharp lobes hold
tainted I'll strap pathos back
that love comes to this ecto-morgue
& ties on craving & passion
but face I loved —
die! die! I'm the woman who loved
a woman who lost

turn it around
I'm the woman in charge
the woman who never succumbed
woman off the couch
woman up and about
I'm the organizing woman
I'll put this place under my spell

I'm the woman who drives
the woman who drove to Siliguri
I'm the woman who walked to Nepal
I took a train to rest my weary limbs
I'm the one who took a sponge bath
the water was cold
another woman soaped my back
I'm the woman slept upright in a cave a hundred years
I'm the woman over the next peak
I learned to drive on the Peak to Peak Highway
    all my signals intact

I provided fresh fuel to the hikers
fed children from my milky breasts
I rode the crest of my own wave
I thirsted for books, books
I took a plane to not calm my nerves
I rode a boat for expediency's sake

I'm the chopping-wood woman
the woman with the axe
I'm the trailblazer
I clear the woods
I take out my own mind

I can out-boast all of you
I can scribe my heart
I thrive on passion
I hang out my shingle
    in business for a night

I'm the ribcage woman
the ribald woman
the beribboned woman
the woman can taking a ribbing, can you?
I'm the imbibing woman
I'm the woman revived
the survivor
the insider woman
the woman who provides
the plied woman
the stymied woman

the woman under clouds
the woman under shrouds
the woman breathing inside her house

I took a trip
woman-left-home
went out to see the day
what would come
what the day would bring
walked among the buildings
walked among the power fronts
inside them: men organizing money
walked on inside neighborhoods
out on the street all kinds of women

I'm the dressed-up woman
the creased woman
the lethargic woman
the sprightly one

wave of woman-future, I ride it
(she conjures long life, fire, tantrums)
no my mother was intellectual
But I'm the body woman
books are sane
I'm the head-in-a-book woman
the travailingest fingers typing are mine
classiest accoutrements, smart talk here
with me it's pleasure weather style
one note of Thelonious Monk is mine

I'm the five senses woman
outings in any town I'm good at
long legs all mine
particular jab
rub at the edge
I'm *not* sentimental
I'm the clever woman
standing in for tolerance
standing outside whim
move over
I write books
I write more books
elegant fibula
parallax sensibility
sleek
fondling
all the world fits in my mouth
I'm the multiple-universes woman

my hair sparks desire
my mouth breathes holy fire

mahakalas roam the yard I inhabit
dakinis sit on my shoulders
elephantine rage
vajra nipples
mistress of the keyboard
no slut to life
I'm the woman who dreams
I'M THE ARTIST INSIDE HER MAGIC HOUSE.

"FAST SPEAKING WOMAN"
& THE DAKINI PRINCIPLE

As I began to write "Fast Speaking Woman," I had in my head that I would do a list-chant telling all the kinds of women there are to be, interweaving personal details (how I see myself: "I'm the impatient woman," "the woman with the keys") with all the energetic adjectives I could conjure up to make the chant speak of/to/for Everywoman. Chant is heartbeat. Chant is an ancient efficacious poetic practice. One of the oldest European chants is the *Song of Amerigin,* a Celtic calendar-alphabet, found in various Irish and Welsh variants, which has such lines:

> I am a stag: *of seven tines,*
> I am a flood: *across a plain,*
> I am a wind: *on a deep lake,*
> I am a tear: *the Sun lets fall,*
> I am a hawk: *above a cliff,*
> I am a thorn: *beneath the nail,*
> I am a wonder: *among flowers*
> I am a wizard: *who but I*
> *Sets the cool head aflame with smoke?*

This also resembles the Welsh *Cad Goddeu (The Battle of the Trees)* with its ubiquitous litany:

> I have been a drop in the air.
> I have been a shining star.
> I have been a word in a book.

I have been a book originally.
I have been a light in a lantern.

I wanted to use this elemental modal structure to capture Everywoman's psyche. The "bottom nature," Gertrude Stein calls it, of any human. But in this case, I was focused on my own femaleness and, by extension, any woman's. There was an unprecedented tidal wave of strong women writers and artists coming to the fore on the American cultural landscape. Any woman might be thinking, saying the same things I was to say and name.

I wrote down a list with all the "A" words in a notebook, beginning "I'm an abalone woman" to "the artist inside her house." I wanted to assert the sense of my mind, my imagination being able to travel as artist, maker, inventor. To see beyond boundaries. The poem arrived in distinct sections with more sound associations than anything else mnemonic, thus "D": defiant, demented, demimonde; "S": solo, sapphire, stay-at-home. Then simple, quick, almost childlike associations, letting the drive of the repeating assertions take over. Naming, that was the thrust. And the chant was to be spoken, or sung, or even more interestingly, *sprechstimme,* spoke/sung.

I was downtown-white-New York-young-sophisticate-college-graduate bohemian, but a real poet too, reading books, writing books, listening to jazz, dabbling in psychotropic drugs, magics, beginning an apprenticeship in tantric Buddhism, attracted to shamanic energies of all kinds. I was already "director" of the very oral-based Poetry Project at St. Mark's Church In-the-Bowery and was reading poems aloud, protesting the war in Vietnam, improvising and working collaboratively with other artists and musicians.

The litany continued on a trip to South American in 1972, a voyage that triggered an abiding interest in Latin American tantra. Tantra literally means "continuity" in the Tibetan Buddhist sense, and relates to the quick path of practice, or Vajrayana, whereby initiates work to overcome basic ego attachment in this lifetime. Working to cure one's own psychophysical being, synchronizing body, speech, and mind. Recognizing the suffering we carry and need to transmute. Powerful demonic visualizations are invoked and mantras sung to invite the energies in. In the Native American context, tantra refers to the unequivocal energy, magic, and healing properties of human mind and sacred language, and the unbroken continuity of enlightenment as well. The fierce images one sees in Olmec, Toltec, Aztec, Maya iconography are not unlike the fierce shamanic deities of Tibetan Buddhism; the legends and myths handed down in one wisdom tradition resonate with the other.

Comrade poet Michael Brownstein, with whom I'd traveled South, brought me the Folkways recording of Maria Sabina, Mazatec shaman, which had been recorded the night of July 21-22, 1956 by V.P. and R. Gordon Wasson. It included Sabina's text, translated from Mazatec into Spanish by Alvaro Estrada and Eloina Estrada de Gonzalez and into English by Henry Munn. He knew I would be gripped by it, and could "use" it, appropriating shamelessly, as poets do. Fired by her potent voice—both the sound and sense (in translation)—I interwove many of her lines, and picked up on the refrain "water that cleans as I go," using it as a place to pause and shift rhythm and acknowledge the cleansing impulse of the writing. Neither shaman nor psychic healer, I was a product of my generation, ignorant then of "cultural colonialism," and eager to learn from other/wiser cultures. When I meditated or took peyote or tried to imitate Navaho chant I heard on recordings, I did so not to co-opt but to "taste" as a timeless seeker in my own imagination's interstices, passionately in love with the magics of the phenomenal world.

Sabina's work comes out of chaste vision. The sacred mushrooms speak through her as she guides young female initiates to confident womanhood and into the Mazatec healing lineage. Her litanies are of radical empowerment. Like highly realized adepts in Tibetan Buddhism her consciousness manifests in many directions simultaneously. She's in all the corners of the universe. Her body of chants (as transcribed and in translation) is clearly one of the great transformational language texts of any time.

My own composition, pale by comparison, is merely exploratory—a bit like Gertrude Stein's "Lifting Belly"—impulsive, free associative, naive. I didn't want to use Sabina's lines literally but to absorb the experience of her work and let it re-emerge in kind of intuitive "re-working." In my early public readings I would often add or improvise lines for the particular situation. I remember a reading for the "street people" of Boulder, Colorado, in 1974, which was held in a park, and the organizers hadn't secured the proper permit for a public gathering. I was in the midst of reading the poem when I saw two cops approaching from a distance, and as they closed in I ascertained that they were both women! I immediately sprang to "I'm the blue cop woman," "I'm the woman with the billy club," "I'm the powerful bust-cop-lady assigned to close this reading down," and so on. I was able to dispel the tension of the situation and complete the performance.

Alvara Estrada's book, *Maria Sabina: Her Life and Chants,* is both an invaluable ethnographic text and a heartbreaking account of the adulteration of a sacred practice. By 1975 the impact of outside visitors to Huatla was great, as it had become fashionable for vision-seekers to make the trip to imbibe the *hongos,* the mushroom-saint children, source of her vision. Estrada's transcription of Sabina's own explication of her difficult life and the subsequent karma that resulted after her healing practices became publicized and abused is a document for these dark times. At least the poetry of Maria Sabina remains, a poetry that still has remedial power, as the best poetry does.

Here is some of what she says about sacred language and healing and wisdom:

> At times the Wise Man sang, sang, and sang. I didn't understand the words exactly, but they pleased me. It was a different language from what we speak in the daytime. It was a language that without my comprehending it attracted me. It was a language

that spoke of stars, animals, and other things unknown to me.

*

The Book was before me, I could see it but not touch it. I tried to caress it but my hands didn't touch anything. I limited myself to contemplating it and, at that moment, I began to speak. Then I realized I was reading the Sacred Book of Language. My Book. The Book of the Principal Ones.

I had attained perfection. I was no longer a simple apprentice. For that, as a prize, as a nomination, the Book had been granted me. When one takes the *saint children,* one can see the Principal Ones. Otherwise not. And it's because the mushrooms are saints; they give wisdom. Wisdom is Language. Language is in the Book.

*

Language makes the dying return to life. The sick recover their health when they hear the words taught by the *saint children.*

I cure with Language, the Language of the *saint children.* When they advise me to sacrifice chickens, they are placed on the parts where it hurts. The rest is Language.

*

Language belongs to the *saint children.* They speak and I have the power to translate.

If I say that I am the little woman of the Book, that means that a *Little-One-Who-Springs-Forth* is a woman and that she is the little woman of the Book. In that way, during the vigil, I turn into a mushroom—little woman—of the book . . .

If I am on the aquatic shore, I say:

I am a woman who is standing in the sand . . .

Because wisdom comes from the place where the sand is born.*

Since the first publication of "Fast Speaking Woman," I've taught classes on shamanic and ethnopoetic literatures at The Naropa Institute, using, among other texts, Jerome Rothenberg's *Technicians of the Sacred,* as well as Sabina's imaginative chants. The class one year tried out various enactments of words to create a force field of energy for protest demonstrations at Rocky Flats plutonium plant in Boulder. One evolved into an antinuclear work that was subsequently performed as a group piece. I also began chanting "Mega mega mega mega mega mega mega death bomb—ENLIGHTEN!" the summer of 1978, later working the lines into lyrics for a "new-wave" recording of "Uh Oh Plutonium!" The constant decades' pressure by poets, artists, and other concerned individuals on the Rocky

*From *Maria Sabina: Her Life and Chants* by Alvara Estrada. Santa Barbara, CA.: Ross-Erickson, Inc., 1981.

41

Flats issue led to numerous exposés, an eventual "bust" of Rocky Flats itself (!) by the FBI, and subsequent disclosures and public involvement.

In some respects the whole shaman concept is problematic, considering the hardships and trials of indigenous practitioners. Poets are hardly shamans, a critic exclaimed. They're jetsetters, bunglers, indulgent egomaniacs! No doubt, I retorted. Poets don't claim to be enlightened curanderos, but sometimes, making themselves available as "antennae of the race," they might receive or tap into energy sources we are usually impervious to. I remember the delight I had when I began "Fast Speaking Woman," thinking every woman can do this, every woman *is* doing this. Like the dakini principle in Buddhism, Everywoman *is* a dakini or skywalker who changes the world through the play of her imagination. She is both messenger and protector and embodies the qualities of compassion, emptiness, and sagacity.

HAG'S HEART

Pre-Adamite sun pours down on aged stones & ferns
(my hag's heart sings these things)
Roof patched with stinky tar, not old but . . . looks shabby
Turn-of-the-century miners' ghosts haunt these canyons
    flecks of mica & gold sparkle in geezer eyes
Nyingmapas—ancient Buddha-Ones—sit in neolithic
    caves mumble vernal formulae to keep the orb a-spin

See a five o'clock shadow
Hear the noon shadow
new shadow, old shadow
Touch the eye's shadow
Write down the noun's shadow
Smell shiny grass

My telephone wears a modern long-shadow face
Wears a rhinocerous face
The clock's faced is tuned-up, staid & wise

The mind's a relic, a fossil, antiquated soldier
The mind's a crone, a dowager

My body is unprecedented, maturing
My mind is antediluvian
My hag's heart scowls at this waning planet
It speaks of its viridity, its crispness
    in the mist of fustiness

The sink is rusty
The city—left behind—is seedy
Threadbare tapestries, worn friendships
obsolete lovers

This hag's the dernier cri of fashion
She's almost bald

That one's outmoded, an anachronism
He's perfectly medieval
She's an Assyriologist

Hag sends the Patriarchs running to their shelters
All graybeards retreat
I am the newest addition
I am the poetry veteran
Please take all the tins, glass, paper & aluminum cans
    & return them to themselves
A succulent voracious appetite sucks the poor old earth
    to fuel the fire
    to mass produce these things
It's too late to be innovator, in-the-vanguard
    Promethean
    except in the mind
A hoary antiquarian nods, as if in assent
Useless things pile up to tip the earth
& my hag's heart gets heavy with these things.

I BOW AT BODHGAYA

I bow at Bodhgaya
Prostrate all around Mahabodhi Temple
Circumambulate on my knees
One prostration is worth a thousand!
(—what young Belgian nun said in
Darjeeling—seeing my greed for enlightenment)
I've just embraced a guru who said Do these
100,000 times-various-practices,
then come back
I'll show you the secrets of the universe

I say it dutifully:
I take refuge in the precious Buddha,
Dharma, Sangha
Give up personal history, imagination,
hope, fear
parents, relatives, lovers, friends,
worldly goods, ambition, my quirky poetry
all grandiose megalomaniacal plots to save the world
& do these prostrations for numberless sentient beings
who for countless suffering lifetimes
were once, each one of them,
or will be,
my very own mother
AH

I inch around the temple with light of Asia in my eyes
irritated, knees bloody, aspiring to what crazy wisdom?
Old Tibetan lady in Darjeeling said
this would be good for my figure—
Was she Buddha in guise of hag,
or Mara tempting me to
future vanities?

A sweaty "hairy bag of water"
I rest under the Bodhi Tree
descendant of one Tathagata
sat under—upon an inscrutable
diamond throne—
his Vajra daughter.

Bodhgaya, India / 1973

RED HAT LAMA

red hat lama's hat is a big flat flame
red hat lama bops your head with ritual vase
   adorned with iridescent peacock feathers
red hat lama, matter of fact
red hat lama performs tirelessly for all sentient beings
red hat lama never fusses
red hat lama adjusts his maroon robes with great
   aplomb with spark in his eye, with darting eye
red hat lama's thoughts pierce like an arrow
red hat lama scratches his chin
red hat lama gives you a basic Tibetan lesson:
   "labu" means "carrot," "turma" is "spoon."
   "ga-u" is "bowl," "shingdong" is "tree"
red hat lama gives teaching mudra—palm extends to
   the universe
red hat lama kneads the tsompa dough
red hat lama makes you hurry: this life is short
   practice! practice!
red hat lama lights incense with savvy grace
red hat lama inspects the American carpenter's molding
red hat lama designs handsome wooden box for his
   bell & dorje
red hat lama teases noisy crow
   throws little stone at Buddha crow
red hat lama proclaims mind as direction
red hat lama closes eyes for divination
red hat lama contacts a restless spirit in the Bardo

red hat lama ordinary, red hat lama not so ordinary

red hat lama clambers up rock sockless in old black
shoes

red hat lama eats no meat

red hat lama sits on earth floor

red hat lama with close-cropped grey hair

red hat lama's face like fantastic rock, weathered by
fierce winds, burning sun

red hat lama high in the Himalayas

red hat lama's eye out window

red hat lama gives out presents

red hat lama suggests you gaze into magic mirror lit by
flame what do you see?
    I see a Neanderthal woman & mountain very
    blurred

red hat lama far away in Darjeeling, far away in
Parphing

red hat lama close in my heart

red hat lama's teacher was a woman

red hat lama wears the hat of yogini Sera Khondro

red hat lama not a tulku

red hat lama long time in a cave

red hat lama perched on a lotus once

red hat lama with outsized European pen

red hat lama buys up all the fish in Siliguri market on
full moon days & sets them free

O Padmasambhava, red lotus lama

red hat lama averts suffering

red hat lama outside the winds of karma

red hat diamond lama on the cusp of the moon

red hat lama at the center of the mandala
red hat lama hovers above me
   (aways at the top of forehead)
red hat lama to the east of me
red hat lama to the south of me
red hat lama to the west of me
red hat lama to the north of me
red hat diamond lotus lama in mind of me

for the incomparable Jadrul Sangye Dorje Rinpoche
Ghoom, India, 1973

LINES TO A
CELEBRATED FRIEND

I feel me in you when you say where you go next, not
    stopping
Stop!
Quit it, Allen, drop it
Go disappear for a year & meditate
Just be Allen-The-Janitor, go clean the stove at Karmê
    Chöling
Don't be so conventional
Give up idiot compassion
Stop telling everyone what to do, then act meek
    turning it all around, makes me feel bad
Sit up straight
Eat more slowly so you'll digest your food properly
Don't eat that terrible food
Empty that soda pop down the drain
Don't be such an overachiever
You're prodigious we know it
The phone rings, don't answer it
Say "no," I dare you
I challenge you to say "no" to that person right now
    beating on your door with new demand on your
    attentions
Don't be so hungry for young boy meat
When you aren't looking it'll magically appear I
    promise
I love you in business, in exertion, in temperament,

in reconciliation, in gentleness
& I'm so relieved you didn't strangle that Italian youth
   on stage in front of 20,000 people when he
   interrupted the show, or massacre the young poet
   who said he was going to commit suicide leaving
   you as his literary executor with two enormous
   shopping bags of poetry. You were jumping up &
   down like a kid having a tantrum. Don't you know
   this isn't good for your blood pressure?
Please sit down on the sofa
Don't be so cowed & forgiving the next moment
Don't worry about what everyone else is thinking
Don't worry about what everyone else is thinking
   about you
No one's smarter or more enlightened or more famous
For heaven's sake Allen, pull up those baggy pants

NYC, 1975

A BOOK OF EVENTS

In Milarepa's Cave

Sit
the logs . . .
flogging is many lives come together
you will be good, you think
hunger is what you'll never show
pick this nettle
light a fire
your broth is the broth of kings
green is the mouth of the cloth-clad lord
sing your sacred songs — again, again

In Her Lament

spin
spin
the saint is a woman scorned
wash your hair
your skirts
scent your hands with myrrh
say you will never die of love
spin
spin

Home

Circumambulate the house
Make first imprints on the snow
Fix what needs your hand
A wasp won't perish
Let her live

TALKING MUSHROOMS

1
side 1, 7 pm
   can't wait till the part Figaro
      rails against women

                        but have to make
a phone call first

2
afraid to look at
   small white hairy moth beastie
      afraid it won't survive

LIFE IS SO DIFFICULT
           the mushrooms say
& then the opposite
     with a fanfare
about getting up, starting all over again, or
   something . . .

3
(side 2)

they say
         do yr practice
         attain enlightenment,
         learn the names of flowers
         learn our name, they say
         forget yr personal universe or if you can't

at least share it
                    the mushrooms are cute that way
            they tell you what you want to hear

4

& now you MUST see the amulet of Horus
                        the mushrooms say

    magnificent relevance *(tout le monde) (tutti mondo)*
        reminding me
                    LEARN ITALIAN
            the mushrooms say
TAKE UP AN INSTRUMENT
        water the plants
    read (AT ONCE)
        THE ENTIRE OPUS OF EDGAR ALLAN POE & MILTON
    & Balzac's LOST ILLUSIONS (for the 3rd time)
        Call Santa Fe for their opera schedule
        Contact the Hopi Elders & the Niman Kachina
            (July 16–19)
                for ceremonies 60 miles north of Winslow
Call David Young the detective who's in town at
    1-444-5578

    Write to the poets of Germany
            & contemplate Rudrahood (how not to attain it)

            the mushrooms shout these things, the
                mushrooms chorus

More Nicolau Retsina!
    LEARN ANCIENT GREEK (the mushrooms will teach you)

the mushrooms laugh now
    MORE COUSCOUS
make it the way the Arabs do:
    "each companion will accommodate the
    couscous according to his/her taste"

the mushrooms make me want to travel
  the way that bluebird does, just down the
    road . . .
      & moth, moth, the mushrooms want you
      to LIVE

5
Señorita, the poem is waiting
Señorita Poet, the page awaits you

Non più andrai, farallone amoroso,
Notte e giorno d'intorno girando

6
O love, bring some relief
    (Porgi, amor, quale ristoro)

clouds, again & again
    obscuring us from

what fantastic eyes on the other side?
  "Reserve the stock for a thick soup base"
    the mushrooms say in *basso profundo*

You ladies who know what love is
  please see if that's what I have in my heart . . .

the mushrooms make me say this

May I ask a question?

No, the mushrooms shout
    DON'T DAWDLE YR LIFE AWAY

WAKE UP INSTANTLY   TURN THE MUSIC OVER

Nederland, Colorado / 1976

BILLY WORK PEYOTE

A piece of sympathetic magic
for the life of William Burroughs, Jr.
(died March 3, 1981)

keep it moving, Billy   there's some motion
   we're doing   the clog dance for ya
embattled or exalted   motions of fronds.

   these support systems   these rivers falling in &
   through you

you way back deep deep deep legroom not enough to
   sit down & whisper

in your ear Billy   no nova Billy   more nourishment

   Billy we send you these stars dotted on the dotted-
   swiss

a most delicious gray for the senses   here Billy take
   them Billy

take these stars Billy   here Billy take the woodsmoke

      (moving Billy moving Billy moving keep it
        moving)

we send you these scents & pleasure of making a tent

   a tent for wanderers for a wandering soul   lost
     your shadow

here's a body to come back to Billy

                        & for your sake we lie down

in a bundle of cloud & for you we eat this medicine to
    cure

    & puke up again   I vomited for you Billy & the last

3 years come back up to me for you Billy   churn it
                                        around

you are still here for us Billy

                 we three   me   Steven   Reed

in still night I can't sit still jumping up for you Billy

         moving keep moving keep it moving Bill

            corn liquor to get the magic down

demodulation Billy

demon hypodermic Billy

              corrigible Billy

Solomon's seal Billy

it's wobbling Billy

correlation Billy

       stock still

          indelible

     hyacinth blood Billy

      cards on the table Billy

high drama & we're missing you Billy

where ya been Billy boy

looking for you Billy

studying your shank Billy
universality Billy

let it go
passing it around

moving keep it moving Billy moving keep it moving
Billy moving
keep it moving Billy Billy moving keep it moving Billy
moving keep it moving Billy moving keep it Bill

1978

SPEL AGAINST SPECIOUS ONES

that they be doused in hot roiling water
that adamantine speech go against them every time
that glamorous women turn their heads from them
that children run
that if they perpetrate war & famine they rot in hell
that hell be ferociously hot
that they are no longer recognizable or loved
that they get no more votes
that they exude an aura of sickness & scent of doom
that their credit runs out
they are disbarred from the marketplace
that they are banished from the kingdom of poetry &
    music forever
that their seed dries up
that they loll about mindlessly in sad places
Om Banish Ho Hum!—Gone Gone Out of Gentle
    Pathways!

*if they have one shred of recognition for their dark ways
    some of this curse is reversible*

BATTERY

A trio of instruments you love the notes
indissectible & extending small rockets of delight
force to love, be loved, love accelerating
love momentum, the love to travel
we will never agree the world contains
so much phenomena we'll put on glasses
abstract it give it structure make a frame
inversely proportional to the square of
two distances apart
make us a family of celestial bodies that we
be one we ellipse about a warming sun
love that sun
dual nature of electrons heal us o heal us
I would come back not hide be in motion
I would attach myself to home again
I would be sister mother lover brother
I would be father I would be infant animal awesome
I would suffer & become extinct again
I would relight the earth with love
I would be still I would be silent & quake
I would be afraid but not for love for
the many manifestations glowing faces
Love the notes as they pour like water
love the water under your feet & when
you look look with eyes of love
all the layers, the ground under
your feet & under the ground

the imagined creatures
& above your feet the grasses the
watercress so fine to eat &
see the roots & bottom of pleasure
of moss look into pleasure the color
disappearing or changing the light
love the light & see the sky the scaffolds the planets
the length the width the distance
the congruity the parallels the fracture
love the body keep it elastic
keep it dancing rallying on its own
keep it safe from harm from red tape
& to those next to you be kind be quiet
be exalted be a charm a fusion be a battery
be insistent be an empire be a symphony
& in a moment's gentle passing
& in a moment's violent passing completely
be her be him be them, see the face beneath
the face & see with eyes of love, gaze straight
into eyes of love with eyes of love

On occasion of a Valentine's Day reading,
the Poetry Project at St. Mark's Church In-the-Bowery, NYC

PRESSURE

When I
see you
climb the walls
I climb them too
No way out of the cosmic mudhole!
no way out of the telephone booth
the classroom
the VW bus the igloo
no way out of the
Quonset hut
the tea for two
the greenhouse, the waterproof tent
the motel room, the
split-level ranch house
the hacienda, the chalet
the icy castle
the formidable mountain
the haunted house
the 747
the rickety porch
the lazy afternoon
my mother's house
Emily Dickinson's staircase
the hospital ward
no way out of Chicago
or Cleveland or Detroit
no way out of the 60-storey office building

the church, the temple, the mosque
the Long Island Rail Road Station
the A train the D train the BMT
the 9th Street crosstown bus
the rain, the 10-inch snow piling up
outside my window
the refreshingly hot shower
no way out of the poolroom
the bowling alley
the noisy bar
the enormous bathtub
the Chinese restaurant
the delicatessen
the department store
the trolley
no way out of the desert
off the Alps
out of the tunnel
out of the river the lake the ocean the bay
off the skis
out of the arena
out of the spotlight
the movie theater
the motion picture screen
no way out of the barn
the farm, the chicken coop
the stable the hay loft
no way out of the doctorate the M.A.
    the B.A. the Ph.D.
the toolshed, the library

my sneakers
no way out of Africa
off Europe, out of Asia
no way off the jeep
the circus the rodeo
the Donizetti opera
La Fille du Regiment
no escape from Joan Sutherland's astounding voice
or the barking dogs chasing the deer weakened from
a long winter
no escape from the guitar or the cello or the
harpsichord
no escape from the mailman, the endless mail
no way out of the stationery store
the print shop
the newspaper office
the glossy IBM retail showroom on William Street
the poker game
the family dinner
the cocktail party
the birthday celebration
no way out of Christmas, off New Year's
out of Philadelphia, Texas, Independence, Mo.
no way out of the sleeping bag no way no way
no way out of the celery patch
the organic vegetable garden
the ancient forest
the deep ravine
the glistening valley
the starry night

the Louvre
the Met
the numerous art galleries of New York City & L.A.
the simple chat, no escape
the zoo no escape
the coat hangers no escape
the history of Russia no escape
China, Japan
the history of music, no escape
the voices of the Pygmies singing in the Ituri rain
    forest
gamelan no escape
Mozart's legacy
& Satie's
no way out of prison
no way off progress off collapse
no way out of the White House
or the Senate or the Capitol
no way no way
no way out of money
even when you're out of it
no way out of whippoorwills swallows gulls
the swimming pool, Bellows Falls
The Great Chain of Being, no escape
The Magnetic Field, no escape
The Continental Shelf, no escape
The Great Barrier Reef
no escape no escape
the piper cub no return
the next acceptance speech no return

the last hurrah the middle age
no way out of TV, no way off Mars
the moon, the sun's radiant energy
no way no way
no way out of structural anthropology
or brain chemistry
or pain killers or pain
no way off pleasure
the rainbow, no escape
the cab ride, no escape
solar flares, no escape
The World Trade Center no escape
The Amazon no escape
amazing grace, no escape
autumn, no escape
my window, no escape
& midnight stubborn midnight no escape
no return no way off
no way out of midnight
black midnight deep midnight
now coaxing midnight gentle midnight no escape

Lower East Side / 1972

LADY TACTICS

she
    not to be confused with she, a dog
            she, not to be confused with she, Liberty
      she a waif
           she a wastrel
                  she, a little birdie
she, not to be confused with pliable
         she in plethora
                she in blue
she with the pliers, or behind the plough
      she
         not to be confused with a jonquil
she in the imperative
         she the liveliest of creatures
    she, not to be confused with Pandora or plaintiff
      or getting seasick or prim
she, a prima donna
         she a secret she a dreamer
she in full force, she rushing home
    she at a desk or in a book
      she, not to be confused with she, a secretary
she a goddess
      she, not to be confused with the Slovak
she, not a slug
      she in season, she in health, she recumbent
    she recuperating
      she, not to be confused with mutton

she a muse
she on a mission, not languishing
she in the landscape, she in silk
she, not to be confused with juniper
with jodhpurs
she with idiosyncrasies
she in labor
she, not to be confused with the conifer
she in consanguinity
she at long last
she, wind, sea, Pompeii, deliberation, home
she in middle C
she the sharpest
she, obliged
she in distinguished sentiments
not to be confused with sentimental
or sly

NOTORIOUS

known for cutting up
being proud, bratty
the clutter in her head
water gushing
known for unpredictability
known for her relationship to the Pasha
known for her stubborn party line
known for more & much too less
known for hazardous outings &
tipping the precipice in her favor
known for specialties succulent & damaging
known for her mouth, splendid temper tantrums
squeezed head, nostalgic lips & antelope eyes
known for her nonsense hands & big calves
known for laughing
known for her cheerful calves
her naughty taste buds
known for her tongue
& gentian violet
known for the blue watch sleeping on her wrist
mistaken for Charlotte Russe
known for breezes through her windy parlour
known for forays into the jungle, onto the tundra
known for partiality to hibiscus & magnolia
partial to squid
impersonal
known for her topological statements
known for toppling the House of Representatives

MUSICAL GARDEN

Can't give you up, speech, can't stop
    clamoring

Can't give you up, sweetheart, my tender
    chocolate big-lipped love

Can't give you up, all dear ones, your bright
    ears & delicate smiles

Can't give you up, Louis Ferdinand Celine,
    you're obsessed & vitriolic & absolutely
    right

Can't give you up, random motion, lucky choices,
    air rides, dominoes, structural linguistics

Can't give you up yet, rum, the bottle's not
    empty & it's warming me

Can't give you up night mail, telephone ringing,
    talking about Kerouac

Can't give up messiness, compulsion, confusion,
    pressure, misery, indulgence

Can't give you up, memory, & murderous dreams
    in which my being's dismembered

Can't give you up, deanimation love

Can't give up the color blue — never never never

Can't give up Andra Pradesh, weep for India's
    starving, going blind no vitamin A
    so necessary, weep for Pakistani flood victims,
    homeless, homeless, homeless

Can't give it up, a propensity for travel,
    moving speedily to friends at every turn,
    scenes, situations I'm not even needed

Can't give it up, heritage, ailanthus trees,
    radial symmetry, bamboo

Can't give up fertility — no way

Can't give you up yet, best jewels, assets,
    secret notebooks, masks

Can't give you up, dinosaur obsession, my jaw
    strangely prominent with carnivore teeth

Can't give up outrage or outrageous behaviour &
    I'll go dancing & wailing for that!

Can't give you up dreamers, inventors, scientists,
    deceivers, iridescent dolphins
    & especially bottle-nose dolphin with
    mouth like my lover's

Can't give you up, black magic fantasies I'll
    make everyone collapse & revive & they'll
    get wiser

Can't give it up, make time stop

Can't do it, ordinary consciousness, I'm trying
   but it's so hard

Can't give you up, musical garden: Bach, Beethoven,
   Buddy Holly, Robert Johnson, Jelly Roll
   Morton!

Can't give up sitting in a hammock in the Fifties,
   I was a babe enjoying solitude —
   hummingbirds

Can't give you up, canyon dream, I'm in between
   there are turtles & little prairie mutations

Can't give up chiffon, sable, inarticulateness,
   simple solid reason, logarithms, furry
   California mountains, not brooding but
   simmering, zeroing in, conquest,
   retreat, romance

Can't give it up, the proposal closest to my heart,
   signs saying Detective Agency in L.A., stop-
   lights, Mercedes, folk fiddling from Sweden

Can't give up Orissa province, prostrations
   optical illusions, fan mail, trekking old
   Inca trails, greasy Tibetan tea, schedules
   to win & lose by, the phases of the moon,
   firebrand meteors, the Kentucky Derby,
   gambling, the ruins of Pisac Peru with stones
   so red & polished & finally honed I ambled
   about all afternoon

Can't give you up Baltic Sea, migrations, go-between, well-wishing, living on the edge of Harshness Street

Can't give it up, foxy, classy, flashy

Can't give you up books, bees, Latin derivatives, Quechua, stationery, habit, responsibility, squabbling, bubbling on till dawn, metal, plastic, electricity rush, melodrama, poverty, the high life, humor, privacy, cynicism, doubt but no boredom

Can't give you up, solar energy, speech, and more speech & more speech & more energy more sunlight more emergency can't give you up can't give it up yet won't do it won't do it can't give it up yet won't give you up yet can't give it up!

New Year's Resolutions 1974

EMPTY SPEECH

empty city
citizens gone to the sea
empty Australia
Aborigines fade
empty London
empty Paris
empty August
sleepless night
empty valium
empty magic
empty body
no one touching
empty oil embargo
empty survey
empty team of specialists
empty Tokyo empty of air
empty economy
empty jet economy
empty Italian auto industry
empty jail
empty trouble
empty morsel
empty region below the clouds
empty coins & calendars
empty video
empty flower arrangement
empty console

empty glory
empty lottery
empty Chagrin Falls
empty corridor
empty Conquistadors
empty labor
empty slumber
empty multicolored planet!
empty instant
empty inner moon
escape trajectory
empty obedience
empty perfection
empty Hong Kong Harbor
empty medicine
empty Russian currency
hollow druggy eyes
empty intimacy
spineless villains
empty tainted future
incipient lust & anger
empty reptiles
volcanic temper
empty-headed sheep
empty shotgun
empty privileges
empty Mexican crockery
empty glass elevators
disappearing rooftops
self-lubricating motor

empty steel factory
empty army
empty artist
empty contrast
empty technology
empty tents
useless gadgets
empty lunar moths
empty extinction
empty accuracy
empty speed & proficiency
empty living expenses
empty radiator
empty turkey
empty pastoral polaroid
empty impossible
empty manikins
empty flamboyancy
empty Orlando Florida
empty scant doubt
empty anticipation
empty handouts
empty chair & power
empty river basin
empty gloom
empty land-development corporation
empty mild recession
colorless dreams
empty Pentagon
empty allegiance

empty bribes
empty tricks
lost illusions
empty surfaces dissolving
head of words

QUEER HEART

Suck cock, Father Country
be gentle & tender, your mind out of the gutter
Kiss pussy, Mother Country, be tactile & subtle
satisfy the ladies with skillful embrace
Heart to heart:
heart on the sleeve of the person who waits—
heart at the door of a fitful night—
heart in the breast of the snappy cadet—
heart of a woman loving a woman—
heart moving cautiously through monitored cement—
heart stretching to livid extremes—
heart of Sleazy City—woan nobody help?
                              doan nobody care?
heart of wounded love frightened to beat—
strongest surest heart revealed! hayloft heart!
Polaris heart! stylish heart! bristling heart!
juicy flesh! embroiled heart! spontaneous flesh!
flesh of ancestors, flesh from the beginning,
                              flesh returning,
flesh smouldering & flesh burning, loose flesh,
flesh licked, flesh disappearing, flesh discovering
heart flash   mind flash   body flash
blessings on all natural acts

On occasion of Gay Rights Action Coalition Rally

LIGHT & SHADOW

Rest you by this various planet
or lounge in the sky lounge
be my guest I'll take you there
& introduce you around & show
you the sky ropes & the
city maps and the world
as round as a lively face
with head & atmosphere
& the sky as breath and the river
as chant and the sun as aria
aria for breathing and for loving
aria for the dancing light & shadow
light & shadow upon the dancing globe
light & shadow on the child's arms
in a park under trees & towers,
light on the fresh canvas, the painter
on the roof of West 21st Street
under thoughtful shadow,
shadow on spoons in the metal drawer
the zebra plant yearning for light
light for the eyes of Beethoven, shadow
inside the piano, mellow now violent
shadow out of the piano, power in the
light of the violin, sweet strings of light,
shadow under my desk, big black boots in winter,
light through friendly words
on shadowy telephone wires,

light in health & shadow in health,
illuminate moon rocks! knowledge from shadow,
light from darkest handwriting, print as light
and white paper, shadow
light from newly polished floors, shadow
in your smile under heavy lids,
cadenza light, shadow on the line of scrimmage
melodious indestructible Vajra songs!
slabs of colored light on the horizon,
the shadow of the big plane on the ground below
a single light in the mosque, shadow in the carved lace
on Persian screens, geometric light on tiles,
light through stained-glass windows, light streaming
through reels of shadowy celluloid
lights dimming in overworked cities,
shadows in villages, no light but one
butter lamps, the black hole of Calcutta
birds in flight, the elephant's slow-moving shadow
the imprint of Sappho, bird scratches
Haydn's *Mass In Time of War*
Leeuwenhoek's back bending to study microscopic
                                              shadows,
lights from headlights, gels for colored light
silver light, winter day, the sun's in Scorpio
golden light, Colorado desert, the sun's incessant
volcano Cotopaxi gleaming, active shadow
through the molten cone
Venus big as searchlight August 1974, dawn,
& bright as the crescent moon!
dim rings of Saturn, Mars reddish light twinkling

in the dense night
light refracted through cloudy shattered glass,
phosphorus glittering in the Mediterranean
the mineral lightning bug glowing on the farmhouse
　　floor
the owl, slow hoot in the forest shadows,
inexplicable X-rays, shadows on the lung
doubt, despair, danger, beware shadows before a storm
shadow of wide-awake country fly on ceiling 3 AM
chemistry, campfires, insanity, flashlights
Christopher Smart on his knees in mad poetic fervor
Virgil, the unmasked hero
Emma Goldman an open book
more names: Gertrude Stein, Mozart, Wittgenstein,
　　Whitman
Cecil Taylor's white jazz light, wave-breaking fingers
on the black & white keys
white egrets nesting on redwoods, a loud flutter
of big wings, of shadow on the green as they head out
toward the lagoon
ultraviolet light radiating from lupine, shadow of
the insects attracted, preparing to land
blue lights at the airport
shadow I'm wearing of our parting
shadow I'm wearing of our parting
glories in the sky raining down all silver & golden
shadows between fingers, between breasts, between legs
shadows of the monoliths, the monuments
the leaning tower of Pisa, the Eiffel Tower
the Camera Obscura in Edinburgh

quaint shadows of mushrooms, tops of amanita
shining like silver moon in moonlight,
bright red by day
Dr. Anton Mesmer experimenting in the chill wind . . .
Apollinaire drunk, Mayakovsky talking to the sun
Rimbaud, bright youth visionary
Pound's silent presence
William Carlos Williams' "Atta boy! Atta boy!"
St. Teresa, a candle, shadow on the mast
death by drowning, a charmed life
shrouded, umbrellaed, sheltered
light from the Himalayas, the Andes
the brightness of snow, the shadows cast by
mountains, by fast moving clouds, the shadow
of stormy Arabs, surefooted Balinese,
Cicero's light now fading, Galileo's vision,
the long shadow of Jesus, Locke's reasoning
light, Homer's voyaging light & shadow
Aristotle, dark & consuming
the shadow of Freud turning the century
Goethe's elective affinities
Newton's arrogant light
Calvin's stoic light & stiff shadow
poor Abelard suffering under prison's damp shadow
Socrates' wise forehead, Einstein's brain the speed
of light, Aquinas, Plato, Pasteur all
lightbulbs in the brown study, a dark laboratory
Herodotus collecting light: knowledge of
cats, Egypt's black ways & foreign women,
Dante spiraling upward to stars,

Darwin, Rousseau, Descartes all thinking
in their armchairs,
Michelangelo lifting his brush to
paint a body's shadows, Leonardo inventing
contemplating wings of light
Milarepa composing on the snowy mountain,
names names once men who walked in daily
                                light & shadow
with light for the modern world,
without gravity, light enough to float
without sun, no shadow
sun on all the wonders of the world
the pyramids casting their shadow in the morning
the buildings blocking my shadow with their shadow
the light of sound, a KLH, a radio box, magnetic tape
the shadowy TV, sinister propaganda parading as light
a devastated land the sun still shines,
bloodshed on the land, shadow
on the American soul, the diamond spirit
of warriors glinting in the sun under evil glare,
shadows in houses when it's always raining,
light reflecting off pools of rain, shadows
of passing traffic of big fur coats, slender
shadows at the beach, a flame in a room
without electricity, shadow on the page of
Stendhal I'm reading, shadow of your head
against a stucco wall, light in the dreams
of martyrs, shadows from their fiery death
at the cruel stake, light on the crystal on
the brain! shadow at the back of the mind

trying to remember something,
shadow in the mouth, a doctor's light
on the polished teeth, in a troubled ear,
black holes, white holes, silver bullets
light on the edge of night
the shadow of the moon,
an eclipse for the total world
shadows in notebooks in matchbooks
till you open them, in the heart until it opens
to light the eyes of the person you love,
the tall shadow of people of trees of rockets
of obsolescence of plastic of neon of laser beams
of solar flares
the light that turns you around
that shocks that blinds
that draws your hands up to your eyes
& you run for shadow
the light of women radiating with all
their wholeness, with soft ground-control
light, men's light of clarity, penetration,
a shiny helmet, fucking on the edge of
night, night on the edge of shadow,
the innate shadow of cities, the hidden light
of cities, the shadow in the valley,
the shadow the horse makes running
the swift hunter's eyes darting between
light & shadow, the shadow the gull
makes, the crow, the eagle, the vulture
the light glistening on the wet seals
playing on the San Francisco Coast,

the shadows furniture makes
in all the living rooms all across the world,
the shadows huts make, the light absorbed
into clothes, the women in South America
beating their clothes against the rocks
drying them in sun & sitting down in shadow,
the cool shadows of water, fish illuminated,
their colors brilliant in the glittering light
through the clear sea, darting in & out of
light & shadow, shadow from the tender water plants
swaying in the tender light & shadow.

WHAT TAKES:
METHYL ISOCYANATE
The Journey of Estsanatlehi

These notes take their form as a writer's journal. Some days I take a work and perform a kind of meditation around it. This was such an occasion. There are thirty-four transitive verb forms of the word "take" and eight intransitive forms. In the transitive sense, we have the meaning, "To consider, assume." "All I hope is that we may not be taken for excisement in this whisky country" said the noble Keats. Intransitively, "Afoot & light-hearted I take to the open road" sang Walt Whitman.

What takes?
Rather, What It Takes, what sticks, in the sense of "never reject anything," an imprint perhaps.
It "takes," or sticks to "me."
It manifests through the "me" who is writing, speaking and doing it.

Also, the sense of "taking over" or "taken over by": absorption.

What's taken in is also a sense of the vastness. The "proceeds" in other words.

We also have the uninterrupted running of the camera or any recording device.
etc., in fact any duration of time, any measure would be a "take." Who determines the amount of time, how do you time an impression? an image?

"As long as it takes," we say.

Slang of "take" is an "attempt" or "try."
Possibly I'll get this right
on the third

        take, but   probably not
                  I've flunked my driving test
                      two — or is it three? — times.
                "the eating and digesting of it."

What takes is what seems to remain in the absorption,
the mind, the language, or all simultaneously, regurgita-
tion, spewing, *shinganged,* in Sanskrit. *Shingang* is the
sense of being thoroughly *processed.*

So I took my malaria pills and went to India. It took
(traveling time and other durations all taken into con-
sideration) about twenty-five hours. I took some photos
& notes, Bob Rosenthal, my traveling companion and
official secretary to Allen Ginsberg, took everything
down on tape at the three-day poetry festival. I still have
a strong impression of Bhopal of the quite tangible
invisible menace, seeing the slums right up against the
Union Carbide plant, intercut with the photos of people
dying and, in particular, the mass cremation photograph
on the museum walls. Two thousand bodies massed
together and awaiting their fire (two thousand times as
powerful as the burning ghats I witnessed in Benares in
1973). A month before even arriving in Bhopal, think-
ing it was sharp on the part of the Government of India
to invite us to there to a poetry festival. It was obviously
being staged in that place to show us our American irre-

sponsibility or insensitivity, in effect, to wake us up. I was scared. I didn't want to be taken for an insensitive exploitive wealthy American. I didn't want to face the horror. Which was in fact not the case, but did happen anyway, to take the sight of suffering home. The sight of old people & children with eyepatches, and speculating on the deformities of generations to come. And where were the doctors? We send lawyers instead. But a month before, I'd written in the long poem that is "including everything" something about Margaret Thatcher, the Iron Lady: "The world gone mad in suffering who's listening? A figurehead is speaking figuratively. You suppose, one of them says, we are facing Armageddon, perhaps not and then it's tasted lethally, in *methyl isocyanate*, its name lethal—hear it? *isolation, cyanide, meth, carring the sound of death,* make this agony never let you sleep & if you do you dream only of death, for it will haunt you until you transmute it and give up your energy & send it hither to anyone any person any country where in pain."

Not meaning to sound gruff but was chilled by this news
      and then   A poetry festival in Bhopal?
                         This seemed a contradiction.

The three-day festival in the outdoor amphitheater began with Vedic chanting by four master pandits, a concert of three Baul minstrels from Bengal, and a mock Meria, or human sacrifice ritual dedicated to the Earth Goddess Dhartani, performed by Kondh tribals who come from the densely wooded hills on the east coast of

India along the Bay of Bengal. The Bauls sang:

> My life is a little oil lamp
> Floating on the waves
> But from which landing pier
> Did you set me afloat?

The Kondh tribals sang at the first mock stab by the priest:

> The Gods wanted this sacrifice
> Earth-goddess wanted this sacrifice
> Let the goddess be happy
> Let her bless our actions

The second night we heard a Pandwani concert, which is a spontaneous rendering of the *Ramayana* with song, music, and gesture, performed by Jhaduram Dewangan and Party. The third day was entirely devoted to poetry readings by twelve modern Indian poets reading in Hindi, Kannada, Malayalam, Assamese, Marathi, Urdu, Bengali, and Oriya all with excellent translation.
Poets writing in English as well.

I also took back with me from India
the stuff of which dreams are made:
Large cities, acid rain, magical lush palms & other succulents, dark guides, and a dream saga in which my child who is fair & blond is abducted & transformed into an intense little beggar child, covered in soot, a lonely rag draped over a scrawny shoulder.

The plane had taken off in the middle of the night and fol-
lowed the sun for twenty-four hours, I arrived in twilight
and stayed in a twilight realm myself between sleeping &
waking a week, dozing off in the
middle of a meeting, a dinner. Then
waking in the middle of the night, passport gone,
unable to get on a plane, long poem stolen, and the man
named for the enlightened king Ashok wants me to take
off my blouse and my underwear, too, which has turned
to rags. . . . . I experience "fear" too.
                    This is called "jet-lag"
In fact Everyone was named "Ashok," and we were
hosted by "Ashok Travels."

My painter friend Michael Criswell in Boulder had come
up with this made-up definition of "ramtil," which I fell
for in a game of Dictionary: "A way of describing the
light from a star that is eclipsed." A ramtil is, in fact, an
African plant grown for its oil rich seeds. A Hindi word,
ramtil from "Rama," Sanskrit for "dark," and "tila,"
Sanskrit for "sesame."

                This took my thinking to Vishnu.
Vishnu, the god of Patriarchal Primordial Vedic Age, is
the principle of light penetrating "Vich" the whole uni-
verse, which he crossed with three steps. It is said that in
the intervals of successive creations, Vishnu sleeps on
the cosmic waters. This explains the alterations of rest &
activity in all cosmic and worldly realms.
This slumber is not death, but a state in which the god's
virtuality slowly ripens to unfold again, as well, in
another universe.

"Ramachandra" is a dark manifestation of Vishnu.

The dark seeds of *methyl isocyanate* suggest to me "a star that is eclipsed."

So what was my "take?"
I felt a mournful timeless, luminous quality, especially in the country, observing the ox-drawn wooden ploughs, and women with brass pitchers balanced on their heads. We took a ride to see the cave paintings at Bhimbetka and delighted in the delicately painted gaur, buffalo, tigers, leopards, elephants, four-horned deer, shaman hunters egging on the chases with prehistoric eyes.

I copied some signs observed after driving around the Delhi streets:

"COOL HOME FANS AIR EVERY CORNER"

"JETGLASS RADIAL
for imported & India Cars"

"LIVE LIFE KINGSIZE"

"RED EVER READY—The chosen One for Your Transistor"

"DRINK A FLORIDA"

"HORN PLEASE" (the buses don't have rear-view mirrors for some reason)

Are these signs the sound of the modern age?

What "takes" are the contradictions, the coemergent qualities of reality.

I had been also working with Native American students at the Institute of American Indian Arts in Sante Fe this winter & spring, and my four-year-old child was confusing the "Indian" of here and over there. "Do all Indians live in India, Mommy?" When I picked up the photos impatient in the car he said "I want to see what an Indian looks like." I had told him of my Navaho students with their beautiful long black hair, and we talked about the Indians as Warriors. The poets of India didn't quite match his fantasy.

Although the poets in Bhopal and my students in Santa Fe (of many different tribes) shared a lot of qualities in their poetry and storytelling, which arises from the oral tradition. My students exhibit humbleness, a sense of the earth & the things upon it as sacred. I observed a subtle, understated, innate appreciation of how poetry can work, and what anyone would want to do with words sounding. And their long inheritance of an oral teaching. The poets of India singing in Urdu & Marathi, that upliftedness that seems to come through tradition, where does it come from?

It seems that People feel a certain way about the world and enact it through ritual over and over again.

Then TV replaced the Zuni narrative story, the chanting in the homes.

In one class at the Institute of American Indian Arts, we wrote after the French poet Max Jacob, and also read John Ashbery's "Litany" and read aloud a performance piece by Jackson MacLow.

I wrote a piece entitled: "Literary Takes":

When you slap my wrist you insult my latest poem, hours of work at the singing machine. I've stopped looking in the mirror, I've stopped traveling to far-away places.

No more shadow today. You have your friends lined up behind you and they say things like *(this is in the Plaza where we can't help but meet on a sunny day),* "You are Amazon in the worst way: waist, bust, eye. Women can't write of rage & fire & war. The woman's a tease in our mouth."

I dream: India is a place in the center of my hand. I hold my hand up to my ear and hear it singing in many tongues.

I sip a Margarita and take stock of the little male band. Will we sit here politely continuing the scabrous collaboration we began? I seem to annoy the text you men began.

"Send the colors back to the sea, where we left our glittering tails, back to the ancient sea," the women sing.

We collaborators disagree, misplace a word, bicker. Writing together as men and women isn't easy.

Now the men have armed themselves with dictionaries. They hide their hooves this way. The plaza darkens now that they've come to literature. We nod & smile at the distance between us.

I made this out of my struggle as a woman and from a dream.
And they make similar works with color, newspaper, satire, gender, and "first thought."

We discuss Navaho language and our entrenched ideas about the solidification of nouns and verbs. Navaho is a language of the verb in contrast to English which relies chiefly on the use of the noun. Navaho is a language of *action* and *movement*.

Nouns receive the flavor of verbs. I mention Gertrude Stein: how nouns are naming (poetry) to her, verbs are narrative and action-oriented and make up prose.
Someone might ask the direction of a certain road, and will be told by a Navaho "It will road him," say, to San Mateo.

"E'atih" means "it roads away to" and thus almost always "doing it so" or "moving it by" is emphasized over "being something."

What does this say about the psychology of the Navaho, or in our contrasting point of view, our own fixatedness?

The Navaho is not interested in time sequences and in defining units of time, but is profoundly preoccupied with all forms of motion. Therefore the Navaho requires great precision in language representation. The structure of the language does not permit the Navaho to be sloppy in presenting types of motion. The Navaho will always differentiate whether the person in question is walking, speeding, slowing down, departing, arriving, traveling with a definite goal in mind, or ambling, moving in this or that direction, traveling on a well-beaten road, whether by foot on horseback, by wagon, car, pickup truck, train, or airplane. Never will the Navaho fail to discriminate verbally between various modes of motion, speed, condition of road & transportation. The burden of this exacting job is always carried by the verb in a complicated system of prefixes, called directional enclitics (late Latin *encliticus,* from Greek *enklitikos*), which carries the sense of *leaning on the preceding word.*

Parenthetically in Tewa—one of the Pueblo languages— the verb is not all that important. The Tewa, unlike the Navahos were a settled people. In our own culture we depend on nouns for exact placement and direction.

According to Navaho myth, man shapes his culture not by being stable but by constantly keeping on the move. These people were nomadic. The flavor of the poetries I was hearing in India was manifestly active, an invocation to energy in motion, not static or preconceived.

The deity most deeply revered by the Navahos is Estsanatlehi who receives her divine status from her ability to transform herself at will. She is The-Woman-Who-Changes. Her task is to keep the universe in flux by way of motion. In an origin myth she is described as "dancing unceasingly from one sacred mountain to the other." In the Navaho faith, "The very act of traveling sanctifies you."

This knowledge resonates with any traveling any woman might do.

Fly to India to hear all the poems you can, and witness the fallout of the Union Carbide tragedy.
It is your duty to take these notes, woman-who-takes.

April, 1985

GYPSY NUN

after Lorca

She wants to be weaving
imaginary *flores:*
magnolia
sunflower
saffron
moonflower
all these for
the *end of time*
In a nearby kitchen
5 yellow grapefruit
ripen
5 wounds of Christ
She doesn't cackle
she gives up her pain
— something outside —
distant — ho —
where did her youth
her sex go?
What reminds her of *what?*
A white dress loosens
Her heart of herbs, sugar,
of spice
isn't broken
Longitudinal pain recedes
further back

20 suns above blink on, off
on, off

She reverts tension to
flowers, horizontal
light playing
a game over her window
blind

>   *magnolia*
>   *sunflower*
>   *saffron*
>   *moonflower*
>   *on, off*
>   *on*
>   *on*

THE NUN ABUTSU

Japan, d. circa 1283

sea wind
 chilly on me
   snow rides down

each night
  look up
    that moon is smaller

I wane
  too
    as I write

not sadness
  brings me
    to words

but how everything
  resembles something else
    is an exultation

enormous waves
  rise —
      flowers! flowers!

the road
  East
    is a song

AFTER MIRABAI

16th century, India

Anne's gone mad she's a mess, hopeless
Gone beyond all help, no return
She beats her drum
She beats her drum in the inner temple
To the sound of the drum she repeats
"Buddha, Buddha"
It's the sweetest melody

A vessel is broken, water is spilled
Her soul she calls "swan" flies away
Anne's body has become alien to her
It's a stranger
Anne's gone mad, ecstatic
She's a mess, hopeless
She's gone beyond all help, no return

She's telling everybody
All through the streets & squares
She says she'll sit at her master's feet forever
She's finally met the master in herself
Now she's Queen of her world

I GUARD THE WOODS

after anonymous Motet, 13th century French

I guard the woods so that no one enters
   if she care not for love
I guard the woods so that no one steals
   a floweret or green branch or pleasure here,
   if she cares not for love
I love so strongly I feel no ill wind   no heat
   no cold   no moisture   no death   no apocalypse
   no obstacle   no famine   no tempest   no flood
I guard the flowers & branches through the seasons

You may not wear a garland of flowers
   unless you are in love.

LAMENT YOU ARE IN THIS MIND OF

after "The Lament Of The Flutes of Tammuz"

Like a lament singing through your marrow all at
     once, like a raging lament, can you hear it? she lifts
     up a lament

She is angry against the wall, lifts she a lament

Exhausted in her white room, she lifts up a lament

Frightened for her child, the child has trouble
     breathing in hospital with transfusion pump, heart
     monitor, oxygen tent, O lift a lament

She breathes into him, lift a lament

From mother to son, she laments she cannot change
     the world

Lift a lament for the rich passion he has

Screaming as they take his blood, lament

He wants the world, he wants to kill it, lift a lament

For guns & swords (they're only sticks) lifts she this
     lament

For tantrums desiring sugar, demanding attention,
     she's lamenting

For his saying in a small cracked voice, "blood,"

"blade," "I'm going to cut off your head," lifts she a
    lament

For he is no longer a baby, lifts she this mother's cry

For he was born in this world

Now tears her hair, now frozen in silence, she's numb

Like a lament the small country has for freedom, lift a
    lament

All people for their oppressors, lift a lament

Lament polluted oceans, poisoned fish & fowl

Lament the stockpiling of endless fantastic—who
    dreams it up?—weaponry

Lament for the demon inside who taunts her virtue,
    ha!

Lament Hilda asleep in cardboard, doorway,
    33 St. Mark's Place

The longing of the chair for you, the book requires
    you

The sun longs to nourish you, the sun could poison
    you

Ethiopia craving water, lift a lament

What does she know about any of this, but she lifts a
    lament in spite of herself

Any mistake, who lifts not a lament?

For all the women who can't control their displays of
heart & tongue, getting into trouble, lift a lament

For all the little colors of personality sneaking out to
fool you, to make the others think well of you, to
entertain you, lift a lament

She misses what was never said to her mother what
might have been said it should have been said &
with this terrible truth she lifts a lament

And to her lover, never said, lift a lament

The ghosts come back to you every time you are in this
mind of won't let it go, no let it go let go lift a lament

Lover to lover: lift it

Mother to daughter: it might be said

Mother to son: I'll say it, lift it, lift a lament

For the mother dying she cried inside Let her go Let
her go, let go lifts she again this lament of let go let
her go, let go

For her cold eyes, cold hands, lift this chill lament

For her heart that kept on going mechanically after it
stopped Let go Let go

for the elder's enlightened eyes — see them again —
white hair — perfect decorum, gentleness, "O do
you think so?" he says modestly
Let him go, 80 years old ready to go, let go

106

Feeling the loss of him terribly

Feeling it unspeakably, he would be amused she is
writing this lift a lament

For his terrible plot to die, lift a lament

Her lament is sexual, it comes from great longing

Her lament could hex the world barren

Her absence causes semen to dry up

Who waits to be born?

The ghosts of the recent dead hover near her because
she can't let them go, let go, let go of them let go

For Beekman Hospital's old men's ward, for the man
with identity gone, no family the nurse said, he
asked me about the Georges — Did they still live
across the street? Could you still buy whiskey at the
old bar just outside there? I am going out the door,
he said, just a nightshirt & old man's jacket on, said
I'm just going out now, old man's slippers, and then
a moment later turning asking Is it all right if I sleep
here, Miss? (gesturing to his own bed)

For my father in the bed next to him, clearer of head,
stronger, better loved but impatient, victimized, lift
I this lament

Like the lament the airplane crashed has for its
destination

Like spinning, radarless in space

We are jerked out of lulling motion constantly to make
lament

I lift it I lift up a lament in October

I lift it in November hard in love

December's lament is full of tears

In January the moon turns away

In February the work continues to lift it, lift a lament

Windy March everything changed

April impatiently misses you, lift a lament

May, June, July, August I traveled away from here

For the mother's face that never concealed its raw love
lift up a lament

Lift a lament for the poet's big body in the Long
Island Veterans' cemetery

For fire wanting fuel lifts she this lament

For her lanquishing body

Her lament is heard through forests

Across oceans her lament is heard

She lows like a beast as the baby is born

She gives birth to suffering over & over again

She lifts up a lament for the endless spinning of Let go,
   let it go

She wants to be as big as the ocean to sink these
   thinking tears

On deaths of Frances Le Fevre Waldman,
Ted Berrigan, Edwin Denby 1982–3.

BATTLE BEAST

I woke in a terrible light
I needed to name my world
"Fire," I said, "Fire burns"
I said, "Fire could burn me"
"Fire burns wood," I said
"Fire warms me"
"Fire cooks," I said, singing
a song over a dead beast
"Fire saves my world"
I moved in such & such a way
(demonstrates)
throwing my head back
& took a hop & two steps to the right,
throwing my head back, and took
a hop & two steps to the left
I circled around the fire and repeated:
"Fire burns," "Fire could burn me,"
"Fire warms," "Fire could save my world"
The smoke made my eyes water
"Water," I said, "Water cools,
but tears burn," "Water," I said
"Water cools fire," I said
"Tears burn"
I needed to name my world
I woke in a terrible light
I write this in flames
I saw pictures in the flames

Animals coming out of animals in the flames
I saw mountains heaving in the flames
I wrote this in water
I saw my wild face in water
Sharp teeth in water
I woke in terror of the letter "F"
I woke in wonder to the burning letter "F"
I wrote it on the earth, on the ground
I took a stick & drew a line like my spine
I crossed it at the top to extend an arm
I crossed it in the middle in order to walk
It looked like a weapon
I walked toward the fire
I woke in bright light to name "Fire."

ANARCHY REGGAE

It touches wire   scares up a storm
(anarchy anarchy anarchy)

Headlines   unrest in capital cities all across the world
(anarchy anarchy anarchy)

Emma Goldman The Red   read her life book in 1974
(anarchy anarchy anarchy)

Going on in a fascist world   continuing this day in
Germany
(anarchy anarchy anarchy)

The death of Peter Kropotkin

The death of Voltarine deCleyre   and more, and
more

Emma Goldman still buys flowers for the love of
beauty!
(anarchy anarchy anarchy)

For the general good we might die
(anarchy anarchy anarchy)

Suicide on occasion & less & less articulate
(anarchy anarchy anarchy)

Appreciate all the ideas   some of the words
(anarchy anarchy anarchy)

"No leaders are good leaders"   "Thrift"   "There is
no god"

"Better no heart than a heart of paprika"
("anarchy" "anarchy" "anarchy")

Take a Boddhisattva vow to liberate all sentient beings
(anarchy anarchy anarchy)

Make a motto "revolution is revelation"
(anarchy anarchy anarchy)

And more   & more   & more & more middle class
(anarchy anarchy anarchy)

A NARC IN ANARCHY where there once was an ARC

Having had an existence of many years, show me how
it works

I'm feeling classical

Arouse & destroy   Anarchia from Greek rulerless

Anarchy   Anarchy   Anarchy

Dear Delicious Anarchy: MANY DARK COLORS.

BARDO CORRIDOR

I had my ego & two grams of hash
Sat down in a corridor
Sat down in a spook-light corridor
in a rueful space
in a jewel-tight box corridor
city night space corridor
in a creature corridor
corridor of pyramid dream power

Well I had my ego & two grams of hash
sat down in a Toltec corridor
in a farewell-medicine dance corridor
in a swift dust storm corridor
in a sub-atomic plenum corridor
in a Bardo corridor

I had my ego & a wounded heart
Sat down in the angriest Bedouin's corridor
In a slum landscape tenement corridor
Demon taking my breath away corridor
in a blazing war-scarred corridor

Well I had my ego & two grams of hash
Sat down in a sinking sun corridor
in a neurological pain corridor
in a bright light corridor
corridor of Bardo dream power

I had my ego & an aspiring heart
Sat down in a Buddhafield corridor
in a prajna paramita corridor
in a boddhisattva's endless-continuum corridor
in a rising-in-the-east-woman corridor
in a corridor of pyramid dream power

I had my ego & I wanted to sing
in I-never-slept-that-way corridor
in a single-minded corridor
in a scepter-of-the-deities corridor
in transcend-this-passion corridor
in a wrathful-mantra corridor
in a wearing-out-of-the-syllables corridor
in a Bardo corridor roar roar ROAR

VERSES FOR THE NEW
AMAZING GRACE

The grace of all the bards who pen
Their words do transport me
Sweet vowels & consonants strengthen
Goddess Poesy's legacy

Heart-pearls roll off the poets' tongues
Who chant in praise of Love
Troubadours blest with hearty lungs
Esoterics zapped from above

Sappho's bite & Shakespeare's wit
& Dante's mystical climb
Dickinson's rhyme, bearded Whitman's breath
Are etched in genetic spine

And if the planet cease to spin
Sad universe go silent, dark
Ancient poetry's echoes will make a din
Rekindle the primordial spark

O I bow down to Christ's thorny crown
All sacraments meant to heal
The Buddha's smile, old Yaweh's frown
And Allah's consummate zeal

But poetry's a Goddess sent
To save a wretch like me
She strums the strings of life's desperate edge
With her haunting melody.

PRATITYA SAMUTPADA

Do you know this term, my friend?
which describes the coarising & interconnectedness
   of all living things?
If you do this to that, this happens
Or that to that, that happens
Or this to this to that to this to that to that
   to this to this to that to that to that, this happens

The sun shines
The dreamer lies down in a suit of fresh clothes
The rain falls on her book of runes
The book gets wet
The seasons come round again
The weapon she dreams of turns back
   on her in the hands of the person
   she never considered in her plot to save the world

Ah, web-life, I bow to the book—
   magical syllables waiting to be caught
I bow to the mind behind it, the tender grass
I bow to the weapon, to the person who wields it
   so it dissolves in the hand

This to that to this to that to that to that to this to that
to that to this to this to this to that to that to this to that

By this merit may all obtain omniscience.

CRACK IN THE WORLD

I see the crack in the world
My body thinks it, sees the gaping crack in the world
My body does it for me to see
Blood flowing through the body crack
Body, send your rivers to the moon
Body twist me to the source of the moon
It turns me under a wave
It sets up the structure to make a baby, then tears
it down again
Architecture of womb-body haunting me
Someone is always watching the ancient flow
It doubles up my mind
Ovum not fertilized
I see the crack in the world
Thoughts intersect in the body
He must not keep me down
Let me go my way alone tonight
No man to touch me
A slash in me, I see the slash in the world tonight
It keeps me whole, but divides me now
Out on land, to bleed
On on street, to bleed
In the snow, blood
This is a South American song
Scent of oleander
Or this is a cactus song
Sing of a blood flower a rose in the crotch

O collapsible legs!
My body enchanted me to this
My body demented to this
It is endometrium shedding
I am compressed in the pressure of my heart
It is life pursuing the crack in the world
Between worlds
Between thoughts
A vacant breath
Words won't do it
Ovum not fertilized
The man hasn't done it
I cover every contingency
the catty one
or puritan walking in a fecund world
Words sing to me of endometrium collapse
Words go down to my belly
Back swelling, to put my body next to the earth
This is periodic
It comes at the full moon
Let me go howling in the night
No man to touch me
Don't fathom my heart tonight, man
No one wants to be around this factory,
this beautiful machine,
but I shun your company anyway
My flexible body imagines the crack
Body with winds
See the crack in the universe
The curse, glorious is upon me

Don't come to my house
Don't expect me at your door
I'm in my celibacy rags
My anthropocentric heart says there's
a crack in the world tonight
It's a long woman's body
It's break in the cycle of birth & death
It's the rapid proliferation of cells
building up to die
I make up the world & kill it again & again
I offer my entrails to the moon
Ovum not fertilized
Architecture haunting me
Collapsible legs you must carry the world
You get away from me
You keep your distance
I will overpower you with my scent
of life & death
You who came through the crack in my world
You men who came out of me, back off
Words come out of the belly
Groaning as the world is pulled apart
Body enchanted to this
Body elaborated on this

Body took the measure of the woman
to explain the fierceness of this time
walking on the periphery of the world.

GUARDIAN & SCRIBE

You are my naming person back of the tongue
You are widower to the terrorist in me
Did she die? Poetry thrives!
You journey to gain profit from my words
You lie under brush, in ambush, I see you
I see you adjust your slim waist, your jangled nerve
I see the spectacle of a beating head a lofty idol
Is life a temple? and we enter & sing these words?
You bow humbly knee to ground
There are many sacrifices here, what's the cost
Claw, hoof, barnacle, sweet slumber
Animal magic, the necromancer's rod
The mouth is a wild wicked deity
Throb of chant, of heart of adrenalin
Makeshift ritual, texts writ in light & blood
Remember a stab in ink, poison pen, lover's quill
Sing, "I am transmuted into dream . . . "
A kiss, one thigh against another, more crazy
mutterings
Work to do! Shreds of work to do! Save the planet for
poetry!
Relief in a body in lover's sharp zeal,
To make sense, pierce the head-scream
I see the flames of your bright ideas leap in the night
And wonder at dark sea heaving under bone
You look anxious the world is threatening
Your brow lightens you are beautiful

Its treasure-eyes carried to the rim of the book
An edge is held discordant in performance
Remind the witnesses to fight but no weapons here
Speak how to release a child under gun
You look bewildered there is no end to suffering
I am poet-messenger, doomspeaking angel
Here is dead poetry's corpse to burn again on the
charnel ground
Millennium's corpse to torch on the holy charnel
ground
Sparks fly out the throat up the page—seeds of future
poetic fire.

MILLENNIUM SUTRA

what learned?
what trigger what reflection?

thus have I heard

This was something I dreamt waking
that the earth could
be scorched galactic cinder
frozen in orbit
about a gone sun

apocalyptic tongue'd preachers
line the mall
with glib glow & twitch
so that you sign on, sign on

give dollars,
& all around children begging
cranium resolve! cranium resolve!

& homeless in the streets
a bed for the night, will work, a bed . . . .

vote apocalyptic
& you will get your war

thus have I heard

rain forests stripped & bare
no trove there
but all you could ever need —
a slump, a dress, a new life,
    tales to be greedy by —
is accessed on a
poison machine

what need we trees?
they grow in the brain

thus have I heard . . .

& SLEEP, THE LAZY OWL
OF NIGHT

a lullaby

& sleep, the lazy Owl of Night

& sleep will make you whole

& sleep, the Bushes of the Field

& sleep will make you grow

& sleep, the Angels in the Sky

& sleep will make you fly

& sleep, my darling, sleep, sleep

& sleep will make you sleep.

(repeat)

"I IS ANOTHER": DISSIPATIVE STRUCTURES

As an artist I am seeking new paradigms. Ilya Prigogine's theory of dissipative structures attracts me as it explores irreversible processes in nature in the movement toward higher and higher orders of life. Prigogine feels that science is essentially ignoring time and that in Newton's universe, time was considered only in regard to motion, as in the trajectory of a moving object. He says there are many aspects of time: decay, history, evolution, the creation of new forms, new ideas. Where is there room for the notion or act of "becoming?" Look at the way nature is saturated with order, alive with pattern: insect colonies, cellular interactions, pulsar and quasar stars, DNA code, memory patterns in human minds, and the symmetrical exchanges of energy in the collision of subatomic particles. At the deepest level of nature, nothing is fixed. Patterns are in constant motion. Some forms in nature are closed systems, such as a rock or a cup of coffee, where no internal transformation of energy occurs. Open systems, on the other hand, are involved in a continual exchange of energy with the environment—such as the ovum and seed or the various life forms and structures that make up a town. Prigogine's term for open systems is "dissipative structures." All living things are dissipative structures. I am a dissipative structure—a flowing apparent wholeness, highly organized but always in process. The more complex a dissipative structure, the more energy is needed to maintain all its connections. It is exceedingly vulnerable to internal fluctuations. Connections may only be sustained by a flow of energy; the system is always in flux. The more coherent the structure, the more unstable it is. This ironic instability is the key to transformation. This dissipation of energy creates the potential for sudden reordering. This does not have to be a slow process; it allows for spontaneity. In my view this is also the potential in poetry and in the performance of poetry.

The continuous movement in a structure results in new fluctuations, which is how I characterize the act or event of extending the writing back off the page. Poetry is not a closed system for me experientially. The elements of old language patterns come into a new one to make new connections. Individuals and societies have great mental and physical potential for transformation as well. *Life eats entropy.* I am interested in the power language has, and particularly in how I use it out of this female body and awareness to change my own consciousness and that of the people around me. I enact language ritual as open-ended survival.

I am interested in extending the written word off the page into a ritual vocalization and event, so that "I" is no longer a personal "I." I enter into the field of the poem with my voice and body. The poem that in turn has manifested out of my voice and body. There is a reciprocity of energy involved. Sometimes as I create the poem, I dance it. It moves through me. Then it takes a shape on the page, which is at first somewhat chaotic. I try to catch the shape as it flies—the text appears as graph, script, sometimes resembling hypnogogic writing. It often rushes on as energy pulse. It might come as an empathetic experience with a particular time, place, or being. The making of the poem, the form it takes both on the page and in its ritual enactment, is an open system involved in a continual exchange of energy with the environment. In this aspect I feel linked to those dancer-shamans in the Paleolithic who identified themselves metaphysically with the untamed creatures that were their sustenance—organisms that were also inspirations and seemed in their various qualities to mirror aspects of the human sorcerers and the community they represented. One wished back then to summon the beasts for food. One needs now to summon the energies for spiritual sustenance, to honor the energies as sustenance and as fields of knowledge. One also admired their prowess and strengths: eye of hawk, radar of bat, ability of reptile to grow back limbs. In the Franco Cantabrian Caves of Le Trois Frères, a 15,000 year old image of a Sorcerer dances above a gamboling tangle of beasts. The Sorcerer presumably enters the realm of Chaos for the greater good, crosses the *limen* (the threshold), descends to the realm of Death, and returns to the middle realm to tell of the experience. This enactment results in a public poetry—a communal poetry.

I want to address specifically the word-workers whose roots are in poetry, and also in the performance of poetry, who view enactment of text as a necessary component of the writing. Obviously there are crossovers of all kinds. Amiri Baraka calls the artist a "cultural worker." As cultural word-worker, I cast my lot with the poets who have a very distinct lineage: those who are allied to Lesbos (the fountainhead of Greek song) in the seventh and sixth centuries BCE. Sappho (approximately 612 BCE established her cult on the island of Lesbos, and her school predated Athens, the high point toward which Greek civilization was heading. What is so extraordinary is the modernness of Sappho's poems—her fragments, really. The women whose names are mentioned in her poems perhaps were her pupils in the religious exercises of Kallichoron Mitylene, or "Mitylene of the beautiful dances." I am drawn to the view of Sappho as leader and chief personality in an institution of poetry and aesthetics because it activates a paradigm in my own life: the poetics school we've founded at the Naropa Institute, the Jack Kerouac School of Disembodied Poetics. Sappho's school however was specifically a Moisopolon Domos, a house of those who cultivated the Muses. This house was primarily concerned with the cult of Aphrodite, and its members formed a Thiasos or cult—which excluded men. The members of a particular *Thiasos* were bound to each other by bonds of intimacy. Maximus of Tyre compared the relations between Sappho and her disciples or pupils with those of Socrates and his. The motives of bonding were in part religious, and all the Muses were honored along with Aphrodite. These ceremonies demanded songs, and Aphrodite's devotees were trained by Sappho. There were a surprising number of women poets in sixth-century-Greece suggesting the acceptability of a life for them in pursuit of the arts of music and dance. Sappho's "style" of writing (what we glean of it) is peculiar to her age and to the Aeolian lyric tradition. It is presumed that she sang or recited her poems with lyre accompaniment, and the poems in turn were passed on to professional singers who sang them wherever Greek was spoken. The earliest papyrus text we have dates from the third century BCE, about three hundred years after her death. We know of Sappho's pupils through her own fragments. What interests me particularly is the notion of poetry and song being linked to communal ceremonies, to celebrations of Artemis and Aphrodite, and to the notion of propitiation. Also fascinating is that women were writing out of their own experience which is linked to an energy field, in this case the ground or "battlefield" of Aphrodite. We also know that Alkman, who flourished before 600 BCE and was the founder of the Dorian school of choral lyric poetry, trained and wrote for choruses of girls in Sparta. One of his *parthenion,* or choir songs of girls, is still extant. I write and perform with this knowledge, scant as it is, this touchstone of the work of Alkman and Sappho. I choose a hypothetical version of Sappho's life, in particular, that activates my own inspiration and power.

Consider the origins of the poem in the fertility survival rites of ancient Greek, where the poem is truly an enactment. There is such a discovery in Crete of the "Hymn of the Kouretes," a very early ritual hymn, sung

131

by a band of armed dancers as they invoke their leader the "Greatest Kouros." They invoke this strapping male youth to "manifest" as they dance for the crops—leap for the grain, fruit, and fleecy flocks. It is basically a celebration of themselves as young, potent, and virile which in turn acts as efficacy for the creatures summoned to "perform." They invoke their leader as lord of moisture and life. They call him "Lord of all that is wet and gleaming." They are the prototypes of all Satyrs and Seilenoi, Sahi, and Maruts of Europe and Asia. They are the early versions of mummers and sword dancers. I remember waking one early morning on St. Mark's Place in the Lower East Side of NYC to a fully costumed band of mummers performing out my window with chant and flute. They danced a kind of glorious, celebratory round. They created a sacred space for a time inside what was then and still is an intriguing although somewhat "degraded" neighborhood.

The cult of the Kouretes, according to Jane Harrison, were at home in Crete and were initiated by a "Mountain Mother" and became symbolically her consorts, her husbands. Marriage was a "mystery" rite. One married the "essence of woman," the uncompromising nature of female energy. One paid obeisance to the most powerful aspects of female energy as well as the accommodating principle. The ceremony secured both fertility and the health of the land. It seems that what shaped the group was the comradery of the community. The poem or hymn arose out of the collective need and served efficaciously, most likely producing the desired effect.

Everyone had a part—this was important and made the whole construct spin.

It would seem that the spheres of poetry and "religion" or sacredness combine wherever an imaginative fusion of the elements of actual experience (which comes to life in words, images, sounds) and a faith or focus in reality that both transcends and sanctifies the experience, are both actively present. My words are empty unless they "connect" with a field of energy that confirms or activates further the breath of the poem. From some point of view, all experience is sacred. The act of the poem I consider sacred as well, not in the theistic sense, but with the commitment that the poem honors the world in all ten directions.

A rite, religious or secular, is an action redone, a commemoration of an original efficacious event, and yet if performed properly, it recharges that original event, and may manifest with the same power and effectiveness. It is like putting a plug in a socket. The so-called divinity or energy being charged or invoked is not separated out from the participants. The leader (actor, sorcerer, performer) is simply an extension of the group and is the embodiment of the collective and creative urge. He or she may be replaced by another "chosen" vehicle or transformer. The performer in the sacred rite cannot be said to be worshiping god, rather the performer experiences him or her, dwells inside him or her. That performer "manifests" or takes on the god or goddess. The old pattern makes the new connection through reenaction.

Jane Harrison, in *Themis* talks about the two basic religious rites: those of "expulsion" and those of "impulsion," or stated more simply, getting rid of evil and securing good. Evil is hunger and barrenness. Good is food and fertility. The Hebrew word for "good" originally meant "good to eat." By analogy, I suggest that poetry is "good to eat." Aristotle said that poetry had two forms: *praise,* which stems from the rites of blessing and induction and comes forth in hymns and heroic poetry, and *blame,* odes that arise from the rituals of riddance and expulsion, and become iambic satire. One such expulsion rite is the ceremony of "Driving Out The Famine." A household slave is driven out of doors with rods of *agnus castus* (a willow-like plant), and over this poor scapegoat are pronounced the words "Out With Famine, In With Wealth & Health." This ritual resonates with the practices of other cultures. The Tibetans practice "tonglen," a sending and receiving practice where the adept breathes in poison and exhales sanity.

Hélène Cixous speaks of "writing the body" as a kind of ritual practice for women: "Woman's body with a thousand and one fiery hearths, when—shattering censorship and yokes—she lets it articulate the proliferation of meanings that run through it in every direction." Biologically, women seem to have a ready access to a construct of multiple meanings, like a multifaceted jewel into which the light pours from myriad directions and out into myriad directions. One meaning points to the hearth, to the goddess Hestia—only one possibility. Others join in praise of Artemis the archer, with her self-assurance and hawk's eye—a perfect markswoman to emulate. These swift protean goddesses keep the wheel "turning." I mention these things because I am hungry and curious about the transcendent qualities of energy, both masculine and feminine. I write poems to Ninni Zaza (an Akkadian goddess of "scripture") and to the Navaho She-Who-Changes, Estsanatlehi. I'm also working on a long poem entitled "Iovis" that addresses many aspects of male energy. "Iovis" is a generative form, the possessive form of the word in the act of owning. Jove or Zeus or any procreative male deity is presumably filling up the phenomenal world with his sperm. He rules through possession, rape, and through the skillful means of the shape-shifter as well. From the psychological point of view (as a "daughter") I need to call him out, reveal him, challenge him, stomp on his corpse, steal his secrets. This long poem also examines War in its many forms.

Making performance out of writing is a way to activate what needs to manifest and has been latent, abused, hidden. Power is invoked through being in touch with all the physical/psychic areas that have been previously unvoiced. I believe there is a "deity" for every possible state of mind. In Buddhist practice, or sadhana, there are elaborate preparations involving invocation, visualization, and liturgy that describe various deities and their powers. Then there is an invitation or invocation to them to "descend." There are two levels of deities in Vajrayana Buddhist: the Jnanasattva and the Samayasattva. "Jnana" literally means "wisdom," and

135

"sattva" means "being." "Samaya" means "coming together" as well as referring to "sacred word" or vow, which is a basic principle in Vajrayana Buddhism. *Samayasattva* is what you create by your visualization. Although something descends, the *Jnanasattva* is not considered an external or divine being that possesses you like a ghost. It is your *own sanity* possessing your visualization. When you visualize, you might be on a trip of some kind, but when the wisdom body descends, you are "untripped." What you have imagined becomes a *real* vision. It enters and embodies the practitioner.

Poetry seems to arrive through a similar process. I set up the space, clear the ground so to speak, re-do habitual rituals. I can feel the poem coming on. There are simple, quite ordinary activities that activate the process, such as glancing out the window, turning on the radio, rereading an evocative text, noting the light, hearing a voice on the lawn, seeing the words "That went by; this may too" copied from a daybook (this is the last line of a poem by the exiled poet Deor, unique among Anglo-Saxon poems for its end stops)—this kind of information propels me forward. Or scanning the daybook again, the notes I jotted down in Oslo at the Viking Ships Museum suddenly become more alive: "Man knows little," a carved rune. What does this mean? Humankind is ignorant? I accept this. Man as opposed to woman knows little? Imagine a ghost ship buried fathoms deep—only these words remain as a kind of rune. Words do this. Now I will unlock them. I remember waking from dreams where words had been thrust

136

on me for decoding: "sluice" was one, another was "matriarchly" which became a poem title. Something gets released, relaxed, and then triggered. I'm not as conscious as I once was of room, or desk. I start the poem. Some "other" thing seems to be writing it for me. A relationship exists between what I only imagined and what comes up as language. There is a working cohesion existing through years of doing. The process becomes one of a glorious meeting of the intangible me, a bundle of conglomerates, everything I can bring to it, everything I know and have experienced to this point, the five senses, the knowledge of how sound might work, and an attuned ear that comes from years of listening to poetry and prose and hearing it in mind's ear. I have empowered myself!

When one is in the grip of a poem, one is contiguous to chaos, yet one maintains a balance, an articulation through the form, or "text," mouthing those very specific vowels and consonants. One pays attention to the smallest increments of speech—phones, phonemes, allophones that register in all the parts of the body. Through language one is making gestures that ward off death, that honor the earth, that encourage the rain to fall or someone to fall in love with you, to stop the war, to close down Rocky Flats. Language provides access to the poet's ultimate desire and its manifested efficacy.

Yet what does this have to do with performance in the current sense? This word comes from the Middle English "performen," from Norman French "parformer," variant of Old French "parfornir." "Par" is the intensifier, from Latin "per" + "fornir," furnish. The word "perform" stresses skill or care. It is the third dictionary meaning after things such as "to begin and carry through to completion" as in "perform an appendectomy." "To take action in accordance with the requirements" is next, and finally we get to "enact a feat or role before an audience"—"to give a public presentation of." There is utilitarian sense here. Synonyms are "execute," "accomplish," "achieve." "Furnish" suggests a kind of perfunctory duty to provide something beyond entertainment, or implies a mastery or attainment of a particular kind of wisdom. The word "rite" or "ritual" emphasizes the scared aspect and is associated too heavily with religion. "Oral poetry" is appropriate but neglects the possibility of gesture or dance. Ed Sanders has come up with the term "perf-po." He writes:

> The time of perf-po is now
> The time of perf-po is now
>
> How beautiful is the
>   unification
> of word & melody   throb & vision
> sky & thrill   perf & joy
> in the 4-dimensional poem zone
> All the components that
> Aristotle listed:
> Plot, diction, Character, Meter/Melody,
> Thought and Spectacle
> fly into the zone

with Music, Motion, Logos,
    Percussion, Bird Songs,
    Clogs, Images,
    Story & Theme Events

    & speckle-throated lilies
        soft on the face

The time of perf-po is now
The time of perf-po is now

I hunger for thee
O perf-po

I yearn for a rinse of nonsense
to click upon my ears

I seethe for the undisappointed dash
of vowels & dithyrambs

I cry for a moan zone
of eery eeryismus

I know
that the words must
star in the mix

and I scheme with every cortical curl
to honor the sonnet, the breath, the bee, and the
lyre

but I hunger for thee
O perf-po

And the time of perf-po is now
The time of perf-po is now

I like Sanders' acoustical awareness, his classical homages and the recognition that the words must shine, that the poet is brought to performance through the words. The "dithyrambs" he conjures here are irregular poetics expressions suggestive of the ancient Greek "dithyramb," the frenzied and impassioned choral hymn and dance of ancient Greece in honor of Dionysus. I would agree that the poem is in fact four-dimensional in its performance.

"Performance poetry" is a useful term I once resisted for its theatrical and entertainment implications. That the term might imply rehearsal, memorization, not allowing for the spontaneity of the occasion seemed problematic. The atmosphere of the space, the audience, the time of night or day, the phases of the moon, the last-minute choices, and also the sense of necessity, that one does this to keep alive, all contribute to bring down the *adisthanas* or blessings of the peaceful and wrathful deities by exemplifying them. As I understand it now, all particulars may enter into and influence the poet's "event." There is an opportunity for chance, spontaneity, improvisation, as well as the "givens" of audience, arena, and so on. My plan is never a fixed one, but a sketch of possibilities. Ideally I like to have a lot of the text spread out on a table before my eyes so that I may select pieces in a random fashion. Sometimes I choose to work with musicians and dancers in a way that leaves our timing undecided until the actual performance.

I attended some of the early happenings at New York City's Judson Church and other places in the 1960s. Performances involving music, props, dance, spontaneous oral text, as well as written text. Proscriptions for movement. Often a multi- or intramedia situation utilizing film, video, props, other voices. Often spontaneous. The Grand Union, of which Barbara Dilley, Yvonne Rainer, and Douglas Dunn were all part, had this exploratory multimedia esthetic as well, although these collaborators were primarily dancers. Carolee Schneeman's *Meatjoy* was an early "happening" in which naked bodies cover themselves with slabs of meat in a wild orgy of flesh and blood. It brings to mind Dionysian rites. The audience feels the event viscerally, energetically, or as in Kerouac's words, experiences "the wheel of the quivering meat conception." I have observed and participated in the dynamic ritual enactment atmosphere of countless poetry events: from Gregory Corso's streaking during a Michael McClure reading, to the symbolic shooting of Kenneth Koch during a reading of a poem entitled "To My Audience" at the St. Mark's Poetry Project. A poetry festival I attended in Bhopal, India included a Khond ritual that mimicked a ritual slaughter. A definite exchange of energy between poet/performer and his or her "muse" as well as an exchange between poet and audience was taking place in all these instances.

141

I attended a performance of Karen Finley in New York City (Finley, more of a performance artist than poet in the traditional sense, has in performance a resemblance to poet John Giorno's style and also to the preacher tradition, carney circus woman and the like). She was performing in a former church, now a club on Sixth Avenue. It was an extremely hot August evening, and the audience had been waiting a long time outside. A cult-like fervor pervaded the atmosphere. There were fans there who had been following her every artistic move. On stage, she immediately worked herself up into a frenzy. She seemed inspired by her own blasphemy as she peed on numerous venerable plaster saints. Her humor was both flagrant and foul. She intoned a kind of physic diatribe. She was handing out pictures of various canonized Saints to the eager audience in a reversal of piety. People grabbed and clutched at them frantically. She was signing the names of the saints to them with a great flourish: Saint Teresa, St. Bernadette. She was drenched in sweat. She had also covered her body with Mazola early on and "performed" masturbation on stage. It was a cathartic and iconoclastic event to say the least. A rite of flagellation, of assault, yet extremely satirical and humorous at the same time. She is most definitively "writing the body" in much of her work. Her work outside the context of performance is tough, unadorned, and poignant. It obviously arrives out of a psychological need to expel demons.

The poet/performer is an "open system" in Prigogine's sense and the vehicle or "scapegoat" in the

Greek ritual sense. These performers have a public appeal for obvious reasons: their work corresponds to a greater need and they dissipate and expel the energy on stage for the rest of us. We are able to participate in the situation vicariously. The resemblance to a sports event should not go unmentioned. Performance for me personally is to be on the spot and available to whatever arises in the environment. It can be a political act or a contest of sorts. The poet Charles Olson spoke of the poet being on the battlefield of Mars. It is a necessary act for me. It is an aspect of the poet's duty: her call to "enact." It is what I know best, it's also all I can do. "Let me try you with my magic power," I say in "Fast Speaking Woman."

I performed pugilistically in a poetry reading using the metaphor of the boxing match. The main event of the Taos Poetry Circus is the World Heavyweight Championship Poetry Bout, consisting of ten rounds of poetry presented as a boxing match with referee, ring girl, bell, and a trophy. Because of its structure and the aspect of "battle" or competition, the event has a highly participatory character. The audience is free to behave the way they might at an actual boxing match — shouting, jeering, spitting, hooting, booing, whistling. The structure permitted, in fact required for its success, these kinds of responses. As contestants, both Victor Henandez Cruz and I pulled out all the stops, egged on by the fury of the mob and by our own sense of drama, display, and incantation. He blamed the full moon for my success especially during the ritual enactments of my menses dementia poem, "Crack in the World," but he took everyone to the point of ecstasy with a spontaneous transformation of the elemental word "mud" to "God." It was a dance of wits, stamina, of energy playing within, around, and for us. In the final round we had a crowning spontaneous poem. People had actually bet money on the event.

For me, reading aloud brings the words off the page. My voice is the key instrument in this act. The voice is the character or characters—all the personae and deities. But I'm interested particularly in exploring the nuances of sound that manifest different states of being. I'm interested in the atmosphere created when I chant, "Make it to me to me to me to me," running the words "to me to me" very close together in a vocal crescendo, or "Mega Mega Mega mega-death-bomb" in a decrescendo, or stretching out the vowels with "Long Long Long to get to One Taste," "lon-on-on-ong, Lon-on-on-ong, it took long to get to one taste," or "CR -A -A -A -CK in the world" so that the "crack" is actually felt and activated, or taking on the phrase "endometrium shedding" in a visceral way. I play with all five vowel sounds in the word "endometrium." The syllables also carry their own semantic message— "end" "o" "me" "trium" (which sounds like "triumph") paralleling the composite word (endometrium) which sounds like its literal meaning "the mucus membrane lining the uterus." As I intone the words "endometrium shedding," I am reenacting that process. It is an "end" "of" "me" and yet a "triumph." I have been told by people in the audience that the enactment of this poem completely evokes the condition and the power of that condition.

Poetry is a kind of *siddhi* (Sanskrit for accomplishment) or energy. The poems that arrive for "performance" (or those that have performance possibilities) seem to manifest psychological states of mind as well as states of energy. This is what attracts me so passionately to Vajrayana Buddhism, because this level of study and practice *engages* energy. It examines in detail *how it manifests*. Yet the poems or writing pieces (chants, monologues, harangues) make their own demands. Often they (the words) take me through a process. The piece, the event, the poem is an active process. *It* is what speaks of. *It* is the experience. *It* is the energy. If these states of mind weren't actualized in performance, I'm not sure how I could handle or contain them properly.

I date my empowerment or confirmation of a life in poetry, not simply my own, to Charles Olson's reading in 1965 at the famous Berkeley Poetry conference. At one point Olson says:

> No, I wanna talk, I mean, you want to listen to a poet? You know, a poet, when he's alive, whether he talks or reads you his poems is the same thing. Dig that! And when he is made of three parts — his life, his mouth, and his poem — then, by god, the earth belongs to us! And what I think has happened is that that's — wow, gee, one doesn't like to claim things, but god, isn't it exciting? I mean, I

feel like a kid, I'm in the presence of an
event, which I don't believe, myself.

"In the presence of an event" was the illuminating phrase
for me. He gave a brilliant talk/reading: fragmented,
disturbed, and chaotic on one level, but completely
lucid on another. He kept the audience there for more
than four hours. Robert Duncan kept begging him to
take a break so everyone could "go pee." Olson said per-
ceptive things like: "You need to know that experience
and society is a complex occasion, which requires as
much wit and power as only poets have." I remember
having an intuitive sense of the man's mind-weave, of
catching the grammar of his thinking, of his synaptical
leaps of thought and insight.

I wrote the poem "Eyes In All The Heads To Be
Looked Out Of" to finally honor my connection to the
poet Charles Olson and that particular occasion in
Berkeley and to express my "birth" as a poet. I wrote
the poem on my birthday as a proclamation of a psychic
birth, also wanting to dissolve the forms through which
the named and declared first person "I"or ego achieve
this. The poem was conceived as a dissipative modal
structure utilizing the architecture of a Balinese temple
as well as evoking the atmosphere of the Tibetan
Buddhist "bardo" (or "pardo") which is an uncondi-
tional space or state of mind without reference points.
This is traditionally the state after death, when the con-
sciousness is without a body to ground it and constantly
comes up against its own mental projections.

This is the poem:

EYES IN ALL HEADS TO BE
LOOKED OUT OF

Formed a new beast today: eye of hawk
heart of lion, radar of bat
Crossed the psychic threshold
the same old old set of eyes
So many layers in one way of working
and you, The Other, you open every one of them
You make me exist, cold by the doorway,
chipper when we don't miss a beat,
despondent for heartbreak's sake
I am the weather when it breaks and destroys
Stroke my sleeping fur, appease me
or I'll deracinate your calm
My Other has shown his many face—
weak, selfish, you see him around woman
I am the idiot too, but will measure myself
against the most beautiful in you
and fail or not, the "I" will come out of joint
I sing on the line for this thinking
of Cambodia devastated continuously by war
The lightening crackles over my head
and turns to angry pellets
Ariadne aux Naxos turns her head
to attack the aria and floats above Libyan

headlines crossing the Line of Death
Someone is waiting for me
Someone is approaching from the opposite direction
I can summon him up, I'll pull off his mask
I got this power when I wasn't looking
between two moments I fell out of
into what was like a noise, a hum
of colored seed syllables that jump on wavelengths
and charge down to the basement to the colored
rooms which only exist to think of feeding Nicaragua
I promise to light more fires fill death
This is the arrogant voice of a thirsty traveler
who came through centuries to meet you
standing in the feeble posture
of the attention position
Yours in the ranks of the Phalanx appearing
now on the tarmac outside: Get in line!
Pick up the weapons: the branches & brushes,
the ankhs, the heart sutras, the wheels of time,
the precious jewels, the precious ministers,
the precious speech
The oppressed and the oppressor can meet at last
and when I heard my old poetry teacher speak
it was like the voice of rain
and I received it always in the guise of earth
Not a guise but gauze that keeps us from each other
because we are two—Me up against the world of you

ALONE ALONE ALONE
SEPARATE SEPARATE SEPARATE

Popped into this illusion to clarify speech
Into this speech, clarify speech
I'm here   I'm here
Too many eyes in one head
I see   I see   I see
I was there I was never there
Eyes in all the heads to be looked out of
No hierarchies but natural ones, nor infinite,
Charles Olson, in the sense of eternal
No such many as mass, there are only
eyes in all the heads to be looked out of
Windows on terror, windows on lovemaking,
on any battlefield, windows on the stars
The gate to the temple is a monstrous
           ROAR
I'll aim this at myself and be it a trajectory
clean to the force of things, look at
me pass under and bow
I BOW TO THE GODDESS OF TEXTURE
I BOW TO THE GODDESS OF THUNDER AND ELECTRICITY
I BOW TO THE GODDESS OF ROCK, OF CORAL
I BOW TO THE GODDESS OF DESIRE AND SELFLESS LOVE
I see this is not arguable as theory
It is refutable
But in the sense I proclaim I see   I see   I see
You can cut me back and I'll grow back on you
Not a curse, this is the way it is
Proclaiming I see   I see   I see
And in this cutting room, cut the root

Cut root torment

Cut sorrow long way down

Cut like chill to bone   Cut

Break off all talk   Cut

Cut root thought
Cut time

Don't cling   CUT

Cut light
Cut it out
Her cut-up manner slays me

Don't fixate on that one   CUT

Cut   heart

and through you and into you   CUT

I'm crazy Miss Linda Longcake
Crazy Miss Linda Longcake
Please come to a white courtesy phone

Cut one hell of a rode   C'est, ça!

Cut the fool of you, the tooth of you

The truth of you, whatever the version

Cut the need of you

The Soviet probes move on from Venus

Cut the quick of you clear of decisions

Cut defense budget blackening oxygen

cut historical action, personal failings

coil ignition of guts in the abdomen

cut animal lassitude
cut carnal money
Cut his presence a demon to me now

in a horse chewed voice CUT

In the voice of the toothless hag Cut

In the voice of "I was a girl" CUT

In the voice of Aphrodite in arms CUT

In the voice of one possessed

In the voice of a small one breathing

through the eye of a needle cut CUT!

The title of the poem comes directly from Charles Olson. His lines "Eyes in all the heads to be looked at," and "No hierarchies but natural ones no such many as mass there are only eyes in all heads to be looked out of" had been resonating in my ear for a considerable time. It conjured the image of the many-headed Tibetan deities—those with eyes in the centers of their fore-head—"wisdom eyes." My idea here was also that the act of seeing (or insight) transcends the notion of hier-archy. Vision produces a sublime democracy. The first lines of the poem speak of being reborn with all my new powers: "eye of hawk," "radar of bat," "heart of lion." The "new beast" is also the poem I am "forming." I am conjuring the various "eyes" and "I's" to gather here under my title which encapsulates and honors the legacy of Charles Olson.

I am also paying homage to William Burroughs, another poet-father precursor who has empowered me over the years with his uncompromising sense of the wicked power and magic of words. Burroughs constructed a mythical superbeast to the delight of his students many years ago at City College in New York. William is a master of dismemberment in his prodigious cut-ups. His beast would have the power to grow back limbs like reptiles, to hear sonically like bats, and so forth. Burroughs is a black magician of words. He understands how the images they invoke when juxtaposed with one another may affect powerful transformations — creating new structures, or new "beasts." This is, in a way, the shaman's task: to take on the powers of the animals that transcend his/her own, to adorn, to proclaim oneself with the skin and hair, the magical implements that both stand in and activate power, to inhabit the personae. Out of the initial declaration in my poem — "Formed a new beast today" — arises the vision to be multiple "I's" or "eyes." I then "cross(ed) the psychic threshold, the same, old, old set of eyes." So although the speaker has the same ancient eyes, they are washed anew, seeing out of the present moment, which has invoked a million eyes to witness as well. This double-sight goes way back. It is primordial, and in the moment of present insight, both past and future dissolve. This is the time of the poem, of the ritual that confirms the presence, the validity of the energy you (he/she) have invoked.

The "old, old" line is also to be spoken in the voice of a hag. Right away the "I" invokes the "other"—both enemy and lover. The "I" wants to challenge, insult, unmask the "other," yet feels the pain of separation at the same time. It then wails, howls its separation "ALONE, ALONE" "SEPARATE, SEPARATE" etc. The voice clarifies out of its longing for other, its duty to communicate, to "clarify speech." The raison d'être of the poem—its only purpose—is this. This leads the adept, after her confrontation with "other" or dualistic reality, to the entrance of the temple whose gate is a "monstrous roar." The loud roar vocalized by the poet unlocks the gate, and perhaps even causes the walls to vibrate and tumble down. It is a pass key, this howl, this "cri de coeur," of existence and birth/death. Once the ROAR is released, is sounded, the initiate, having left his/her "separateness" outside the gate, may now enter the temple. The gate is the roar, and the roar is the boundary that both keeps us out and lets us enter. It is where life and death—past and present—dissolve as well. They become unconditional states of mind. The poet has to enter the final stage, the inner sanctum at this point.

Next the initiate must bow to the four directions paying homage to "texture" (the passing show, manifested phenomena), "thunder and electricity" (the sky/ fire), "rock and coral" (the elemental earth-world which includes the sea), and "desire and selfless love" (passion and compassion (transcendent passion). The initiate has realized his/her relationship and can now move into the transformational phase of the poem. With her "speech" she can literally cut the ties to all phenomena, to all compounded situations and realities as well as meet her own death. She can literally "eject" her consciousness into space. She is the magician, the hurler of thunderbolts. She can literally "cut" in the explosive ejaculation of this word. The word is the seed syllable for transformation. In a sense this "cut" is heard on cellular level. Perhaps certain unnecessary circuits which hinder psychic transformation are severed in the brain as well.

The ritual enacted in this poem resonates with the "chöd" practice in tantric Buddhism. Here the adept literally dismembers (through visualization) his/her own body. The energy is dissipated like an agape feast, in which one shares the body, symbolized by food. One can pass through fear this way. As I conceived this poem, I bowed, I screeched the word "cut." I let it come out as I heard it in my own body. The litany of the various personae/stages for the female all proclaim their voices, their "cuts."

The eyes from the earlier stage of the poem have now become voices. It is said that hearing is the last of the senses to dissolve after death. The "I's" have become transcendent. They are a full circle, an energy construct that coexists as hag, girl, "Aphrodite in arms" (meaning armed, bearing weapons), one "possessed," and a "small

154

one breathing through the eye of a needle." This is a miracle, that the consciousness (the "new birth") can pass through the eye of the needle. The needle's "eye" is also one of the many "eyes" to pass through—eye here as window, gateway, entrance. The last "cut" dissolves the poem, dismantles its power and propels it into the void. The poet-initiate has come full circle. She has "formed a new beast" and killed it as well. The beast is the vehicle, as the poem is the vehicle for the energy, the vision, the proclamation to pop into. "Popped into this illusion to clarify speech." It pops itself out as well when it has accomplished its ritual enactment. It has courted, appeased, and paid homage, as well as built its own efficacy of power.

The "cut" on a more mundane level is the film (the "passing show") being halted. The Buddhist practice invoked here is called "stopping the mind," which means stopping discursive, rational, grasping, conceptual mind for a split second. The result is a gap between life and death—between breaths. Does it work? The voices in the poem are manifested as I hear them. I perform them as I hear them. The poem is both a ritual to activate transformation as well as transformation itself. The gate *is* the temple. The "path" *is* the "goal." I re-do in the reading of poem, how it arrived, how it worked on me, in me, around me. The poem retains its energy and may be re-activated again through the performance of it. Song, it is said, predates our own species. There are many pitches, nervous pulses, many variations that predate us, in the insect world alone, for example. I have taken a vow to unlock some of those myriad sounds.

A poem is a kind of textured energy, or a modal structure. The poems I conceive of for performance seem to manifest psychological states of mind. They come together in a mental, verbal, physical, and emotional form — making their particular demands on my voice and body. The poem is an active event on this occasion. It is what it speaks of, what it vibrates, what radiates out, creating a kind of energy field. The performance of the text has power, and animation. I am the "energumen." The poem is the experience. I am not as interested in making poems about things inasmuch as the subject matter is the primary thrust, but rather in working to manifest a complete universe, through sound, emotion, vibration, rhythm, and so on. That this poem is "about" perception, that this is a poem "about" a woman with many eyes, would not be that compelling.

Because the occasion for "Eyes In All The Heads To Be Looked Out Of" was my own birthday, I saw myself at a critical juncture, and the poem became a force field in which to gather up my strengths. I needed to speak its "message" to myself as well as to identify and name in images. I needed, too, to stomp and bow and "kill" discursive thinking. I needed to establish, to demarcate, the boundaries in relationship to the space around me.

The motive for the performance of writing and propelling the poem "Eyes In All Heads To Be Looked Out Of" is social as well as personal. I feel that what I am doing in my work is attempting to propitiate the gods, goddesses, muses, or energy fields, and that what we are doing here in the poetics community also connects to a greater vision. The point is that the work, group effort and concentration, and conversation is active event in time, not a prescription for anything else. It's all happening right here, right now. The experience of ecstasy is a timeless phenomenon, and is available to all of us through our work. The possibility for exchanges of energy through our "open sytems" is a real and exciting one.

The strength of our own "linguistic revolution" of the twentieth century (according to Saussure and Wittgenstein) is the recognition that meaning is not simply something "expressed" or reflected in language, but is actually produced by it. Art is not to be seen as the expression of an individual subject. Rather, the subject is just the place or medium where the truth of the world speaks or enacts itself, and it is this truth we hear. It is an accumulation, a power gathering over time, that bursts forth in song at the appropriate moment through an appropriate vehicle.

I believe feminine energy is (in spite of indications to the contrary) in the ascendant in this culture. We need more than ever to redress the balance. This activity in its many aspects is already an open system. I feel this in my own fluidity and the ability I have to perform my work. For me, an important image called the *Anodos Vase* exists in Gaia worship. This depiction shows a great mountain of earth artificially covered with a thick coat of white plaster or paint. On it are painted a tree, leaf sprays, and a tortoise. From the top of the mound rises a tree. In the midst of this scene rises up a figure of woman. It is a grave mound, an omphalos-sanctuary, and she who is the spirit of the earth incarnate rises up to bring and manifest new life. This is the traditional "bringing up of Semele." Semele, Earth, never went to heaven, she rose up out of Earth. When Patriarchy comes in, she takes a lower place and has to be fetched up. Orpheus as the lover fetches up Semele, or Euridice. Women artists rise up. We are on the mound, which is our stage, our platform, a throne for the manifesting deity. It is Sappho's stage. It is an image of "becoming" in Prigogine's definition, a pattern or process which reoccurs and is in constant motion. We no longer have to be fetched up. Nor do we have to fetch for anyone else. This also serves as paradigm for performance. Literally: taking center stage.

Citings & Further Reference

Prigogine, Ilya. *Order Out of Chaos, Man's New Dialogue with Nature*. New York/Toronto: Bantam Books, 1984.

Harrison, Jane. *Epilegomena to the Study of Greek Religion* and *Themis*. New York: University Books, 1962.

Cixious, Hélène (with Catherine Clement). *The Newly Born Woman*. Minneapolis: University of Minnesota Press, 1986.

Sanders, Edward. "The Time of Perf-Po," from *Thirsting for Peace in A Raging Century*. Minneapolis: Coffee House Press, 1987.

Finley, Karen. *A Certain Level of Denial* (CD), Salem, Massachusetts: Rykodisc, 1994.

Olson, Charles. *Charles Olson Reading at Berkeley* (as transcribed by Zoe Brown). San Francisco: Coyote, 1966.

Barnstone, Willis. *Sappho, Lyrics in the Original Greek with Translations*. New York: New York University Press, 1965. (See also translation by Guy Davenport)

duBois, Page. *Sappho Is Burning,* Chicago: University of Chicago Press, 1995.

Barnard, Mary. *Sappho; a New Translation*. Berkeley: University of California Press, 1958.

Burroughs, William S. *The Adding Machine: Selected Essays*. New York: Seaver Books, 1986.

The Battle of The Bards. A Lannan Literary Video. Los Angeles: Metropolitan Pictures, 1990.

Eyes in All Heads. (Anne Waldman performance video). Boulder; Colorado: Phoebus Productions, 1990.

Waldman, Anne. "Eyes In All Heads" from *Helping The Dreamer: New & Selected Poems 1966-1988*. Minneapolis: Coffee House Press, 1989.